The

ULTIMATE WEDDING REGISTRY WORKBOOK

The
ULTIMATE
WEDDING REGISTRY
WORKBOOK

Choosing the Best Wedding Gifts
for Your Life Together

SHARON NAYLOR

CITADEL PRESS
Kensington Publishing Corp.
www.kensingtonbooks.com

CITADEL PRESS BOOKS are published by

Kensington Publishing Corp.
850 Third Avenue
New York, NY 10022

All Kensington titles, imprints, and distributed lines are available at special quantity discounts for bulk purchases for sales promotions, premiums, fund-raising, educational, or institutional use. Special book excerpts or customized printings can also be created to fit specific needs. For details, write or phone the office of the Kensington special sales manager: Kensington Publishing Corp., 850 Third Avenue, New York, NY 10022, attn: Special Sales Department; phone 1-800-221-2647.

CITADEL PRESS and the Citadel logo are Reg. U.S. Pat. & TM Off.

First printing: November 2005

10 9 8 7 6 5 4 3 2 1

Printed in the United States of America

Library of Congress Control Number: 2005928768

ISBN 0-8065-2686-6

For my mom

CONTENTS

ACKNOWLEDGMENTS

Many thanks to Bruce Bender, Margaret Wolf, and Richard Ember, my editors at Kensington; my incredible agent Meredith Bernstein; my tireless and inspiring publicist Scott Buhrmaster; and my creative (and very talented) Web master Mike Napolitan—without you in my corner, this wouldn't be possible.

Also, thanks to Diane Forden, Cybele Eidenschenk, and Lisa Dickens at *Bridal Guide* for their fabulous registry survey results delivered at top speed; and Steven M. Syczewski, Litsa Rorris, and Crys Stewart at WeddingChannel.com and *WeddingBells* magazine for their generous permission to use their wedding registry statistics. Randi Gerber and Dave Novakoff kindly allowed me to share their Just-Give.org registry with you, and for that example of "giving a little bit back," I thank them for being such inspirations. Speaking of inspirations, Bethany Robertson at the I Do Foundation is an angel on earth and generously sent more than I requested—thank you, Bethany! And Amy Stavis at *Tableware Today* made my day with her permission to use the tableware registry survey that graces the pages of the sections to come.

And of course, thank you, congratulations, and best wishes to the many engaged and recently married couples who shared their registry stories with me so that *you* can register to your heart's content as well.

May all of you receive everything you desire . . .

INTRODUCTION

Congratulations on your engagement! You have so many exciting experiences about to come your way: trying on wedding gowns and finding *The One*—the dress of your dreams, walking into the perfect ballroom where you can picture yourself dancing and sipping champagne, slipping those wedding rings on each other's fingers . . . it's all a dream coming true.

Right now, it's time to think about one of the most exciting and enjoyable parts of your pre-wedding plans: registering for your wedding gifts. Words can barely express how thrilled engaged couples are when they walk into a store like celebrities, saying "I want this . . . and this . . . and this . . . and this." It's the ultimate shopping spree, all the better because you're not paying for anything! There's something of a fantasy about the registry experience like no other time in your life: walking among the most wonderful new gadgets and beautiful china patterns, picking out what you'd like to receive as you start your new life.

The choices you make will design the look and feel of your bedroom, your kitchen, your living room, your den, and on and on. You'll use these items every day as husband and wife, your *children* will use them, and they'll become a part of the pattern of your future—that wonderful escape from the world called *home*. And you get to create it right now as if you're painting a picture on a blank canvas.

The world of wedding registries has changed so much recently— it's not your mother's wedding registry! From mountain bikes to home office equipment, gourmet cookware, cashmere bedding sets, backyard patio furniture, even furniture and lighting for your home . . . plus the techno-gadgets your groom is wild about—DVD players, camcorders, TiVo—and registering for gifts is a very exciting prospect, more so now than at any other time in the past.

Vera Wang, Kate Spade, Ralph Lauren . . . but This Isn't Gown Shopping

One reason registries have made such a big jump into a whole new world of excitement is the proliferation of top-name celebrity fashion designers putting their artistic touches on everything from china and stemware to sheets to towels to furniture. Fashion designers, after all, are the epitome of taste, style, and grace. It brings a whole new excitement to your department-store shopping trip when you know you're going to find Vera Wang designs in the Wedgwood and Wallace china patterns; over twenty Ralph Lauren designs among the Mikasa crystal; Oscar de la Renta among the Ginori selection; Kate Spade designing patterns for Lenox. Now, shopping for your place settings can be just as exciting as shopping for your gown. The big names are out there, making the twenty-first-century bridal registry a shopping trip through the elite worlds of fashion and design icons. Especially if you're into fashion, you know that your favorite celebrity designers have an unmistakable way with clean lines and contemporary shapes, sophisticated and stylish classic design, and now they can be a part of *your* home style as well . . . with your guests buying them for you upon your request.

Use this book to guide you as you plan your registry, using the hottest new trends in products and rooms to register for; blending your existing households; and upgrading everything from your kitchen knives to your living room sofa. Ready to begin? Let's get started . . .

Part One

THE NEW TRENDS
IN REGISTERING
FOR GIFTS

Hold on just a second before you start looking at blenders! The hottest new trends in registries will stock your kitchen to a gourmet chef's liking, but they'll also point you in some additional exciting directions.

Like outside. Your back deck can become an oasis for both relaxing and entertaining. You can create an amazing party zone out there, *the* place to be for your family parties and casual barbecues among friends. Imagine a hammock between those two big oak trees where you and your partner can enjoy a warm summer day.

Speaking of your partner . . .

Grooms are the new hot shoppers when it comes to bridal registries, and not just because they get to use that very cool barcode scanner gun to record items right onto your online registry. So what does today's groom want on your list? You're about to find out.

From all the tools to throw a great dinner party to all the tools to add an addition to your home, give your bedroom a makeover just like you've seen on all those extreme decorating television shows . . .

- To registering for kayaks and mountain bikes because you both love the outdoors and your active lifestyle so much
- To using that new loophole about financial gifts (more on this in a second)

The newest trends in registering give you all you need to create not just a lovely home, but an exciting *lifestyle* together.

Coming up right now . . . the trends that will make you both very, very happy.

Chapter 1

Blame *Trading Spaces*

S o tell me . . . what's your favorite home decorating show? If you're like most couples, you've spent some nights watching *Trading Spaces, While You Were Out, Extreme Makeover: Home Edition, Merge,* and all of the other "I Can't Believe It's the Same Room" home redecorating (and sometimes remodeling) shows. You know that "The Big Reveal" is coming. Take a blank white room with mismatched furniture and mountains of CDs and books, and twenty-four hours later, it's a stylish oasis with a plasma screen TV, leather couches, romantic lighting, live potted trees, and a skylight. All for $1,000.

We watch in awe as gifted interior decorators work their magic with even the most cluttered rooms, and then we start looking at our *own* bedrooms, thinking, I want a chocolate brown silk bedspread too, or Hey, I really want to get rid of these yellow walls. Lucky for you, you're the bride and groom, so you can *register* for everything you'll need to create your own delicious home makeover. Minus the cameras, perky host, diva stylist, and hot carpenter out in the driveway.

Even better? You're not limited to $1,000, as some shows' budgets are. You can register for items way beyond that value.

Where does this trend take you? To home remodeling stores like Home Depot and Lowe's with bridal registries all set for those painting supplies and wallpaper borders; that new bathroom sink; those crystal drawer pulls, window treatments, wooden blinds, and finials; those backyard patio sets and wooden swings for your wraparound porch; and even that kit to create a fish-stocked pond in your backyard.

Home makeover and decorating television shows are inspiring, to say the least. From colors to styles to room themes, plus an education from the designers on Interior Decorating 101—like room blocking, lighting, traffic flow, and everything you ever wanted to know about hardwood floors—this is where today's bride and groom are getting their dream home ideas and signing up for the supplies they'll need to build it.

Chapter 2

Give the Groom the Gun

Your groom just loves holding the TV remote. Techno-gadgets are a must on his birthday wish list, and he has more digital *everythings* than some small countries' entire police departments. There's something about the bridal registry scanner gun that grooms love—the power, the control, the point-and-click efficiency. As much fun as it is for grooms to "play" with the scanner gun, that's not the only reason why so many grooms are fully on board for the trip to register for your wedding gifts.

Before we get to *what* these grooms are registering for (and you might be surprised!), let's talk about *why* they're so much more into the process. Here's what real grooms had to say about why they were excited about registering for gifts:

According to *WeddingBells* magazine's recent survey, created in partnership with WeddingChannel.com, 98 percent of today's grooms-to-be are walking through those store aisles or registering online with their brides. Here's how the survey stacked up:

Very involved: 56 percent

Somewhat involved: 30 percent

Not very involved: 12 percent

Not at all involved: 2 percent

- *"Hey, it's going to be my home, too. I want the place to reflect Us."*
- *"We've talked for years about what kind of home we'd have together in the future. We have all these plans. And now we get to pick out everything together, just like we talked about for so long."*
- *"I'M the chef. Between the two of us, I'm the one who can cook and loves cooking. I make her special dinners all the time. So when it comes to picking out the goods for the kitchen, I'm definitely signing up for the great knives, the great cookware, all the tools I'll need. She cares more about the bedroom, so that's all her. But for the kitchen, and she'll even tell you this—I know what I'm talking about."*
- *"This is a house that I'll be living in, so it should reflect my tastes as well. I don't want the floral bedspread or the pink towels."*
- *"We love to entertain at home, so I'm looking forward to picking out the bar set, great martini glasses, and red wine glasses, really decking out our gear for all the parties and dinners we'll have together."*
- *"Why should she get to have all the fun?"*

After all, it's not just registering for gifts that today's modern groom-to-be is excited about. He's helping to plan the wedding as a full partner. He's designing invitations, creating a wedding web page for the two of them, tasting cake samples, auditioning bands, choosing tuxes, and even designing the wedding bands. So, too, is he into the gifts of choice.

As for *his* gifts of choice, grooms are registering along the lines of all the biggest trends, including even the most domestic and traditional of items (like the blender). But when it comes to what they call "the fun stuff," here's what's on their list:

- Barbecue grills
- Barware sets: martini glasses, shakers, pilsner glasses
- Camping equipment
- Computer systems and printers
- Digital cameras
- DVD players
- Entertainment centers

Why Grooms Are Much More Involved with Registering . . .

Diane Forden, editor-in-chief of *Bridal Guide* magazine, says: "More couples are paying for and planning their weddings together than ever before, so grooms are more involved in every aspect of wedding planning, including the registry. I think there is a realization now that these registry items are for *both* of them, not just pretty dishes for the bride. They're setting up a new home together, and guys want some say in the types of items they'll be living with. Also, these grooms were raised by women enlightened by the feminist movement. Their moms worked, raised families, and demanded more of a partnership from their husbands than previous generations. They taught their sons that it's okay for a guy to like to cook, that men should help with housework, and that marriage is working together as a team."

- Gift certificates: music, movies, books
- Home exercise equipment: treadmills, weight sets, Alpine ski sets, ab machines
- Home office equipment: fax machines and scanners
- Home security systems
- Luggage: sets, garment bags, duffel bags, carryons, attaché cases, travel organizers
- Plasma screen or large-screen televisions
- Sports equipment: golf clubs, mountain bikes, kayaks
- Surround sound digital entertainment systems
- Tickets to major sports events or season tickets for his favorite team
- Tools

It's not a surprising list, but these men won't be boxed into a stereotype. They're not only looking at techno-gadgets and tools. Check out this list of survey results from *WeddingBells* magazine and WeddingChannel.com for their preferences:

The Most Expensive Item He Registered For

Tableware: 18 percent

Cookware: 15 percent

Knife set: 6 percent

Kitchen electrics: 6 percent

Furniture: 5 percent

Luggage: 5 percent

Home entertainment electronics: 5 percent

Barbecue and patio equipment: 5 percent

Bedding: 4 percent

Tools: 4 percent

That's right. His top four big-money items are for the kitchen. The electronics are at only 5 percent. So, he's going to be just as into the everyday dishware, the nonstick skillets, griddles, formal table settings, and cutlery as the bride-to-be. Maybe, in some cases, more so.

This makes him your equal partner in registering for gifts. You'll make your decisions together, update your list together as time goes by, and enjoy every minute together.

Chapter 3

The Outdoorsy Type

The previous chapter reported that camping equipment made the most popular list, and that's a great reflection of the bridal registry trend in "taking it outside." Beyond setting up backyard dining areas and party zones as an extension of your living room (more on that in the next chapter), registries are opened wide up to the couple who loves to be outdoors doing adventurous and active things together.

It could be that you love hiking or boating, that you go camping or mountain climbing together. Being active is a part of your lifestyle together, and it's part of your identity as a couple.

Here's some good news . . . you can stock up on terrific outdoor gear right through your bridal registry. Sure, you're registered at a department store for all of those kitchen and bedroom items, but your *other* registry is all about the "great outdoors." Check out sports stores in your area to see if they have a bridal or gift registry. Chances are, with this big trend in sporting gear as a must-have for a growing legion of brides and grooms, they will have a registry set up.

The Top Picks for Outdoorsy Types

- Camping gear: tents
- Hiking gear: hiking boots, jackets, and backpacks
- Kayaks and canoes
- Mountain bikes for two
- Car racks for bicycles
- Coolers

- Handheld global positioning systems
- Walkie-talkie sets
- Binoculars
- Telescopes with star ID software
- Books and guides on outdoor sports
- Golf clubs: his and hers, all golfing accessories
- Tennis racquets
- In-line skates
- And more . . .

If you feel strange about registering for mountain bikes, remember . . . your guests *want* to give you something you'll use and enjoy. The guests who know you best will smile when they see these items on your list, saying, *"That's SO them!"* and they'll be thrilled to give a great item to you. Even better, groups of friends or relatives can go in on those pricey mountain bikes together, knowing that they've fulfilled one of your wishes. Be sure to send them a postcard when the two of you are off on a terrific biking trek or tour of the vineyards! As one of my brides said while lacing up her new in-line skates, "This is *so* much better than a rice cooker or frozen yogurt maker!"

A Top Choice in Outdoorsy Registries

Outdoor adventurers rave about the specialized registry at www.rei.com, where you can find camping gear and other terrific choices for all your future adventures together.

Chapter 4

The Party's at Our Place

Entertaining at home is one of *the* top priorities for newlyweds (notice I said *one* of the top priorities!), and you, too, are likely right within this big trend of registering for items that will help make your parties stand out.

From martini glasses to wine tubs, fondue sets to a hibachi grill, having great accessories makes your dinner party, happy hour, cocktail party, wine and cheese night, or casual poolside barbecue a stylish and impressive gathering for all your most important friends, family, and colleagues.

This is a growing twenty-first-century trend. Brides and grooms say their loved ones are a valuable part of their lives, so they want to share time with them often . . . and at home. Fine dinners at fancy restaurants are lovely, but nothing beats the home celebration. Experts say this is a "nesting" phenomenon that grew in our post–September 11 world: a longing to return to family values, a desire to spend as much quality time with special people as possible, a wish to celebrate big family occasions together, a need to share quiet evenings at home together. We know what matters most, and so we plan to make our time together even more special.

Oh, the Parties You'll Host

Hundreds of brides and grooms listed the following kinds of entertaining they're looking forward to doing in their homes:

- family-style dinners • formal dinners • wine and cheese parties with friends • brunches • luncheons • cocktail parties • poolside barbecues • backyard barbecues

• picnics • birthday and anniversary parties • showers for
friends • family reunions • their *kids'* birthday parties
• girls' night in • surprise parties for family and friends
• gatherings for work colleagues • hosting dinners for
clients • book club meetings

Pass the Chips . . . or the Champagne

Consistent occasion-based favorites were, surprisingly,
Superbowl parties and Oscar parties, Kentucky Derby parties
and Daytona 500 parties, at-home celebrations to share big
events with either large or intimate groups of friends. Most
couples say these parties are rituals for their groups, with them
as the annual hosts. Their friends look forward to this party all
year. Now, couples say, their fun new registry items will make
their annual special event parties even more legendary, and
the shared memories will be that much more unforgettable.

The Big Entertaining Categories

In the realm of entertaining, brides and grooms report that they're
focusing on three major categories: outdoor entertaining, family dinners, and just-the-two-of-us events.

Outdoor Entertaining

Maybe it's the grooms who have a big pull in this category, but an
entirely new block of registry items are the new must-haves on bridal
registry lists. Couples have a wonderful fantasy of hosting outdoor
parties with the groom at the barbecue grill basting a rack of ribs or
turning a slab of salmon, a fabulous patio table set for eight with
Fiestaware place settings and pitchers of sangria, guests lounging in
the sun on Adirondack chairs or starting up a friendly game of volleyball in the yard. The blender whirls and colorful frozen margaritas
are served, and everyone's raving about what a gorgeous day it is.

The Rise in Outdoor Space Registry Choices

Diane Forden, editor-in-chief of *Bridal Guide* magazine, shares stats on why outdoor items like patio sets, barbecue grills, and lawnmowers are showing up on more bridal registries these days: "The registries have expanded to include items for outdoor entertaining and relaxation for a number of reasons. Again, the influence of having more men involved in the registry process can account for the barbecue grills and set, lawnmowers, tools, etc. Also, a recent *Bridal Guide* survey indicated that if they did not already own their own home, 88.3 percent of couples marrying today do plan to buy a home. In fact, 20.4 percent will buy before the wedding, 21. One percent will buy within the first year of marriage, and within three years of marriage a whopping 45 percent plan to purchase a new home. So, they are thinking ahead and purchasing items for backyards, decks, and patios. Also, if couples are already living together and have a lot of the basics, they'll want to register for these items. Finally, I believe that couples see their home as a haven and are eager to create a comfortable, fun environment where they picture many happy gatherings (both inside and outside the home) with family and friends."

This could be the new American dream: the blissful family gathering in the yard and the unmistakable smell of steaks sizzling on the grill making all the neighbors envious.

The Top Bridal Registry Picks for the Dream of Outdoor Entertaining

- A high-quality barbecue grill with all the attachments: rotisserie, separate grill sections, top-notch barbecue tools
- Barbecue "toys": baskets for grilling vegetables and seafood, shish kebab sets
- Hibachi sets

- Casual place settings: Fiestaware platters and plates
- Margarita pitcher and glass sets
- Margarita-making machines
- Ice-shaving machines
- Wine tubs and ice buckets
- Patio table and chair sets
- Portable bars and bar stools
- Hammocks
- Adirondack chairs
- Benches
- Lawn games: badminton and volleyball sets, horseshoes, archery sets
- Picnic blankets and baskets
- Landscaping items: equipment, trees, flowers, bulbs, build-it-yourself pond kits to create a garden border for a true outdoor oasis
- Lighting sets: spotlights, fairy lights to string in trees and on decks and terraces
- Portable CD player for playing mood and party music during outdoor parties

Think about what *you* want for your own outdoor parties, and register at home décor *and* home improvement stores for all the gear you'll need.

Family Dinners

Of course, you'll host your new in-laws for dinner in the future. Family dinners bringing your side and your spouse's side together are likely on the horizon. That first meal at your place can be a harrowing experience, especially if you're feeling pressure to duplicate or improve on handed-down family recipes. *Especially* if certain family members are . . . how shall I say this? . . . hard to please.

Or you could be one of the lucky ones whose family meals and Thanksgiving dinners are pure bliss—cozy family time when everyone helps out in the kitchen, the wine flows, and the conversation is always easy and laugh-filled.

Registering for these family celebrations opens up a world of wonderful gift items, many of which you'll show off at this party. Serving platters, dish warmers, those gorgeous red wineglasses, your monogrammed napkins, table linens, freshly brewed espresso.

You know that planning the wedding itself is just the opening act to a future filled with rich family memories. Your wedding gift registry provides you with all the tools and special touches you'll need to create the setting. And impress the family.

Formal or Informal Party Place Settings?

You'll need to decide whether you wish to register for formal, fine china, or more casual dinnerware. Part of what helps you to make that decision is looking at the types of dinners and parties you plan to host in the future. Will you host Thanksgiving at your place, setting out your collection of fine china? Or will you more likely hold informal parties where a more casual place setting is more appropriate. Some couples do decide that they *won't* need the finest of china, so they register instead for a more casual yet still impressive dinnerware set. Others know to prepare for an unknown future—they register for the casual dinnerware set *and* the formal set. Eventually, you may host more formal dinners and holiday gatherings at your place, so always remember your foresight. Register for who you are now, but also for who you both may be in the future. This collection will last you a lifetime.

Just-the-Two-of-Us Events

And of course, entertaining also means creating special moments and meals just for the two of you to share alone in your cozy couple bliss. Whether you cook for him, he cooks for you, or you both cook together, whether it's a planned special dinner written in pen in your day planners or a surprise when you get home from work, consider the following:

The Top Choices in Supplies for Those Parties for Two

- **Breakfast in Bed.** His and her bed trays with side pockets to hold the morning newspaper; juice glasses, heart-shaped waffle makers, Belgian waffle makers, nonstick griddles for perfect pancakes and just a two-second cleanup, bud vases to hold tiny daisies as an accent on the tray
- **Romantic dinners.** Formal dinner place settings, silverware, champagne flutes or wine glasses
- **Midnight munchies.** A panini maker, fondue set, s'mores maker complete with sterno set, ice cream bowls
- **Picnics.** A cozy picnic blanket and picnic basket, red wine glasses, platters for chocolate-covered strawberries or grapes, storage containers to hold cheeses and crackers

"We love to surprise each other with little romantic moments. He's woken me up at midnight before, bringing me downstairs to a picnic he'd set up in front of the fireplace. He laid out our new cashmere blanket we received at the shower, and we fed each other strawberries. Now THAT was a great night! We just added some more romantic-type items to our registry, planning ahead for more romantic evenings." —Jennifer and Charlie

Chapter 5

Upgrade Me

You don't just want *stuff*, you want the *Good* Stuff.

Perhaps you both already have your own home together, or your own separate places, already filled with such necessities as dishes, everyday silverware, pots and pans, and all the kitchen gadgets you could ever need. Most couples today have a supply of linens and kitchen tools, but they may be a supply of well-worn items you've had since college, or the crockery you took from your parents' place when *they* got a new set of Calphalon cookware. Those bowls in your cupboard . . . you remember eating cereal from them while studying for your finals years ago. Your towels? You've had them for ages. Your microwave works okay, and your steak knives can cut a London broil with a little bit of effort.

You don't really *need* new stuff, but now's the perfect time to *upgrade*.

So, you'll register for the 100 percent Egyptian cotton towels, replacing your "okay" white cotton bath sheets and washcloths with the plush upgrades in rich colors—cranberry, hunter green, or a cool sage green. You'll trade in the "okay" microwave for a powerful one with extra features. Your old coffeemaker gets handed down to a friend while you make room for a sleek twenty-first-century silver model with dual cup-serving spouts, a space-age timer, auto shutoff, and a coffee-bean grinder built in. Those old, worn skillets get moved to the back of the cabinet to make room for an upgraded nonstick set. Your collection of mismatched coffee mugs can hold pencils and pens in your office now, because you're about to get a beautiful set of new mugs with ornate handles and footed bases.

At no other time in your life will everyone you know be willing to upgrade everything you own. Does it make you greedy? No way. You're starting a new life together, and part of the fun is supplying yourselves with great new things.

The Top Items Brides and Grooms Wish to Upgrade

- **Baking pans.** Toss the old versions, those scraped and warped bundt pans and muffin tins, for new, nonstick ones.
- **Knives.** A great set of new chef-quality cutlery will last for years and years.
- **Place settings.** Fine dinnerware and casual dinnerware are wonderful items to upgrade for your new life together.
- **Sheets.** Most upgrades go to higher thread counts and different color schemes, softer fabrics and more luxury.
- **Towels.** Egyptian cotton is high on the upgrade wish list, for post-shower or post-bath pampering.
- **Coffeemakers.** Again, it's the extra features that make mornings a breeze.
- **Food processors.** Chef-style quality and special attachments make your current processor or blender seem ancient.
- **Kitchen gadgets.** Sleek designs in egg timers replace those 1970s-era plastic wind-ups, silver measuring spoons replace plastic, and more modern designs mean your stylish kitchen is impressive down to the smallest details.
- **Luggage.** It's one of the top things couples register for. A matching set with organizing panels and pockets, a matching

---

Luggage on Your List

According to the 2004 *Bridal Guide* magazine gift registry survey, 34.8 percent of engaged couples plan to register for new luggage, while 22.8 pecent of couples plan to buy their new luggage on their own. Only the remaining 31.2 percent are sticking with their already-owned sets.

garment bag and carryon bag for the honeymoon and all future vacations and adventures together. No more banged-up old suitcases. Now, it's a matching *His* and *Hers* set.
- **Other top-rankers.** Furniture, television sets, camcorders, and the good old barbecue grill all make the desired upgrade list.

What to Do with the Old Stuff?

When you upgrade, you'll have a collection of old pots, pans, linens, dishes, and many other things that you might want to discard. If you don't have a relative or friend who's just moved or just finished school, happy for the hand-me-downs, make a call to the local women's shelter or soup kitchen to donate your items. Charities in your area are always looking for supplies, so perhaps you can make their day.

Some Additional Ideas for Your Potential Donation

- Area rugs
- Blankets
- Coffeemakers
- Comforters
- Computer system or laptop (with hard drives erased)
- Cookware and bakeware
- Exercise equipment
- Furniture
- Microwave
- VHS movies if you're upgrading to DVDs
- And more . . .

For Further Design Inspiration . . .

I've spent hours in my hammock flipping through the *Williams-Sonoma* catalog and dreaming of someday designing my living room to look like *that*. No doubt you've seen a catalog or magazine photo spread of a heavenly bedroom set and wished the same for yourself. You may even have torn out the glossy magazine page and stored it in your "someday" file. Well, someday has arrived. Now you can register for the perfectly styled living room, that wispy curtain bedroom, and that streamlined silver appliance–filled kitchen. Inspiration for your future home can come from anywhere. The perfect dining room design can show up tomorrow in your mailbox.

Here are the top places to look for home décor inspiration, for those expert ideas and artistic concepts, colors, styles, furniture layout, and quirky accents, that will add a measure of dreams-come–true to your bridal registry:

In Print

- Home décor catalogs
- Interior decorating magazines, like *Architectural Digest*
- Celebrity decorating magazine issues, like *InStyle* magazine's "Homes" special issues
- Women's magazines' special editions, like *Woman's Day*'s special budget decorating issues
- Your favorite women's magazines' regular design articles, like *O*'s list of "Favorite Things"
- Interior design Web sites
- Hotel and resort Web sites, where you'll see graphics of elegantly appointed presidential suites and outdoor terraces decked out with designer fabrics and fabulous place settings
- Web sites for bed-and-breakfasts, which provide graphics of featured suites, fireplace rooms, outdoor terraces, rooftop terraces, bathrooms, and hot tub areas

In Person

Sure, you can find the ideal decorating inspiration in the pages of a catalog or magazine, or on a Web site, but sometimes there's nothing like being there in person. So, plan a day trip to check out the following, whether you're intent on finding design styles as the reason for your trip, or if you're in the mood for a weekend getaway.

Places to Visit

- Look for design homes, "sample" homes that are shown as part of an interior design conference, showcase, or even the model homes shown in new condominium complexes.
- Attend design expos or conferences, planned in either a major city or as part of a community development program. Check city or towns' calendars of events to find out when interior decorator expos are going to open their doors.
- Visit a nearby Home Depot Expo, the home supply store chain's specialty showcase stores, where professional interior decorators place their orders for lighting, tiles, window treatments, kitchen appliances, and everything else they need to create idyllic settings for their clients. Even if you're not likely to buy a glass shower stall for yourself, you could turn a corner and find the ideal bedroom set or window blinds.
- Join your local interior decorating club. Many community social clubs offer such specialty groups as book clubs, babysitting co-ops, and gourmet clubs, and they also feature interior decorating clubs where design ideas are freely shared by members and guest speakers. You'll learn plenty about the hot new styles and fabrics and perhaps obtain referrals for local tile experts and landscapers, pool designers, and fine finish carpenters.
- Stop in at hotels and resorts, even if for only a drink in their lounge. I've walked into amazing, elegant clubhouses and garden atriums that have inspired me to whip out my notepad and sketch out design ideas for my place.

- If you're staying at a luxury hotel chain on a business trip or during a vacation, look for inspiration in their bedding, their bathroom towels and robes, or their modern waterfall bathtub faucet.
- Borrow ideas from friends and family. A cousin may have the most gorgeous home you've ever seen, overlooking a golf course or a marina. Your uncle's ski home might have that perfect mix of leather couches and cashmere throws. A friend may have perfect decorating sense, so pay him or her the ultimate compliment. When you borrow ideas, that's a big compliment as well—as long as you don't copy the room down to the smallest detail. That's just a little bit scary.
- Take it outside by visiting garden nurseries, many of which showcase sample backyard and border setups, professionally planted and maintained.
- Remember, the same goes for visiting pool stores, where outdoor pool patios are on display along with hot tubs, outdoor barbecue kitchens, and terrace designs.
- Take some time at a spa, soaking in more than just that terrific shea butter hair deep conditioner. You may get design inspiration from the indoor water fountain in the lobby, the bring-the-outside-inside wall of water in the treatment room, the modern track lighting in the massage area, the mosaic tile tables out by the pool, or the calming sage green wall paint in the pedicure salon.
- Go on holiday home tours, even if it's "too touristy." Some communities regularly schedule Victorian home tours, with each stop along the walking path featuring a stately historic home decorated to full brilliance in holiday décor.
- Screen your favorite movies. The major Hollywood studios spend a lot of money hiring expert set designers to create that gorgeous beach house in *Something's Gotta Give*, Meg Ryan's quaint apartment in *You've Got Mail*, or that ideal family home in the Steve Martin remake of *Father of the Bride*, parts one and two. Borrow from the pros (and the stars) by grabbing some inspiration right off the set.

- Watch those "homes of the stars" television specials and regular series and sketch out or write down the ideas that light you up. You might adore a celebrity's lighted makeup mirror or oversized red ottoman used as a coffee table. You may wish to copy a closet organization style or frame your most important achievements in great frames and mats just like the stars do.
- And of course, watch those home redecoration shows we discussed earlier . . .

Chapter 6

Registering for Cash?

B rides-to-be have approached me and asked, "Is it okay if we *don't* register for gifts and ask our guests to give us cash instead? We have all we need, we've lived together for years, and we'd really like to pay off our school loans with the wedding money. Is that okay?"

No. It's not okay. Number one, if you don't register for gift items, your guests will shop according to *their* tastes, not yours. No guest will see your lack of an official registry as a sign that cash gifts are the rule. And you *can't*—under any circumstances, according to long-held etiquette and general common sense—ask guests to give you money. Ever.

But . . .

The new freedoms of modern-day weddings are bending that firm rule ever so slightly. Now, you can set up registries of a financial nature. It may be controversial to traditionalists and etiquette mavens, but the mainstream in the wedding industry is answering the call for finance-based gift choices—contributions to the downpayment for your first home, for instance, and stocks and bonds. Those are the two big financial gift categories right now and are provided in more detail in the following pages. First, let's handle the issue of guest acceptance.

Some people will be shocked to see that you've actually set up a bank account/registry because you want to buy a house. Sure, it makes perfect sense that you do have all the linens and plates you need, and your big goal is to buy a house. That's exactly why these financial registries are popping up all over the place, flourishing, and gaining national and etiquette approval from all the top wedding experts and bridal magazines. It makes sense. It works with today's realities. Marrying couples need a financial foothold and the ability to make wise investments even more than they need a good bagel cutter. Still, eyebrows will raise. That's how it goes when you're on the front of a trend.

Here is how to handle the inevitable feedback you might get, any judgments or condemnations made by guests who don't quite understand that things have changed . . .

If you do wish to create a financial registry, create it *in addition* to a traditional gift registry. For instance, you might announce on your wedding Web site that you're registered at X Bank for a downpayment registry *and* at Bed Bath & Beyond. Guests who don't wish to participate in your downpayment registry can always get you the fine cotton sheets, the wine glasses, or that bagel cutter from your traditional registry. Other guests might opt to chip in for your home rather than have to choose between your towels and your sheets. This is the best way to set up a financial registry . . . giving guests a choice between the two options.

When Eyebrows *Don't* Raise

Don't be surprised if there is *no* whispering, judging, or condemning your choice of a financial registry. After all, many of your guests might be financially savvy themselves, greeting the news of your downpayment registry with relief and excitement—"Wow, that is a *great* idea! I wish I had that when I got married!" Today's brides and grooms report that they brace themselves for controversy and then find themselves surprised to be hailed as geniuses. In some areas of the country, in some cultures, giving cash gifts in envelopes is the norm, so bringing a wrapped gift to the wedding would be the questionable move. It's always a matter of what's right for your crowd.

Home Downpayment Registries

Primarily, these are in the form of special bank accounts, set up in your names as an interest-bearing account earmarked for your home downpayment. The most well known of these accounts right now is the Bridal Registry Account, created by the Federal Department of Housing and Urban Development. You can open a savings account through a bank participating in this program (call 800-CALL-FHA [225-5342] to find member banks near you), and guests can deposit their "gifts" to you either at the bank or online. The funds are then in place for your home downpayment.

You'll find many different plans of the home downpayment variety once you start looking for them. Some plans allow guests to buy American Express Gift Cheques attached to a program for first-time home buyers. Call your bank and ask about any in-place financial registry programs, and inquire about the terms, minimums to open the account, and all other bank-sponsored requirements.

As for notifying your guests, a link on your personal wedding Web site can bring them right to the page where they'll learn all about the program and can participate with a click of the mouse.

Stocks and Bonds

What better gift than investing in your future? Sure, the same applies to contributing to your home downpayment, but the fastest-growing trend in financial registries is helping the bride and groom create a booming stock and bond portfolio. You've read all those financial news stories: invest $1,000 while you're in your twenties or thirties, and it will be worth $650,000 at the time of your retirement. Imagine *that* as a wedding gift. So many engaged couples are signing on, and guests, too, are checking out new Web sites that allow the gifts of stock.

One of the programs getting a lot of attention right now is www.GiftsofStock.com, which is a dividend reinvestment program (aka DRIPs) that allows the buyer to set up the bride and groom with individual stocks and bonds. These are company-sponsored investment programs that let the owner of at least one share of stock re-invest their dividends. As the bride and groom, you can choose your preferred stocks from fifty-six specially-selected companies (at the time of this writing), which were hand-chosen for their good long-term growth and low- to no-cost setup. When someone buys stocks from your program, you'll get an e-mail notice from GiftsofStock.com, complete with a mock stock certificate.

Another program offering a stock-purchase bridal registry is www.RegisterStock.com. Outside of registries (that is, companies who offer the service but not in the form of a bridal registry), you'll

Cash for Your Own Unique Purchase

Some registries also allow you to sign on for cash contributions that you will use any way you wish—such as buying a car or building an addition to your home. While yes, it's still considered "iffy" to ask for cash donations, the establishment of official donation registries is quickly removing that old stigma. The Knot (www.theknot.com), one of the biggest names out there, has set up a "Create-a-Gift" program for just this use, answering the very realistic call from brides and grooms for some sort of officially sanctioned cash gift donation program. Their "Create-a-Gift" registry works like this . . . you sign on to their registry and list the things you wish to acquire with the money your guests donate. It could be portions of your honeymoon, a romantic dinner for two, office supplies, whatever you have in mind. Then plug in as many $50 gift certificate "credits" as you'll need to fulfill each individual purchase. You've just created your own personalized registry. Your guests then shop through your list and make their purchases in the form of American Express Gift Cheques that are noted on your registry and then mailed to you via UPS for your use. The guests can purchase the entire item you selected or a portion of it (like $50 of the $600 that your dream bed costs). Call it a do-it-yourself program, but it's one that gives the cash donation realism and the flexibility that many couples are looking for today.

find stock and bond purchase options at www.Frame-a-Stock.com and www.OneShare.com.

Check these and any other programs out thoroughly before you sign on. Talk to your financial advisor for tax laws and general advice. Make sure you understand the fine print, any requirements for you to buy shares before you register for additional gift shares, and all the financial ramifications for your tax status.

What's the number one change on registries these days? Diane Forden, editor-in-chief of *Bridal Guide* magazine, says this about the biggest change in registries today, compared with those of five years ago: "Inevitably, it's the continued expansion of the registry list and the inclusion of nontraditional items such as luggage, sports equipment, honeymoons, wine, mortgages, stocks and bonds—all of these are available to couples as registry items."

Part Two

SMART REGISTERING
WITH GUESTS IN MIND

Chapter 7

How Many Registries Can You Do?

t used to be that most brides chose one place of registry. Years ago, her mom suggested her favorite department store, and that was *the* place.

Now, brides—and their grooms—are most apt to register at two to three different stores. After all, there are so many kinds of stores and shopping categories (housewares, sports equipment, home remodeling, stocks, honeymoons, and so on), it would be a shame to limit yourselves to only one type of registry.

According to *WeddingBells* magazine and WeddingChannel.com . . .

> 77 percent of brides- and grooms-to-be will register at two to three stores

According to *Bridal Guide* magazine's most recent registry survey (2004) . . .

> 3.7 percent will register at one store
>
> 33.6 percent will register at two stores
>
> 37.3 percent will register at three stores
>
> 25.4 percent will register at four or more stores

The combination of which stores is up to you. You could do one home décor store (Bed Bath & Beyond or Williams-Sonoma) and one home supply store (Home Depot or Lowe's). You could do one home décor and one stock program, or one home décor, one sporting goods store or site (like Rei.com), and then one art boutique store as your third option. (More on local boutique registries in chapter 38.)

Two important things to remember when deciding your registry: (1) The registries you choose must be accessible to your guests and (2) you must be able to fulfill your choices of everything you need, in all the categories that interest you.

"Can We Do Two Home Décor Stores?"

Absolutely. You might love the sheets offered at Bed Bath & Beyond but love the cookware at Williams-Sonoma. So sign up for your chosen items at both.

Registering at two somewhat similar stores shows you know what you want, and guests appreciate having two to three lists of options to scan rather than trying to find something affordable that's still available on your picked-over list. The more options, wherever you find them, the better.

You couldn't be getting married at a better time. Brides of decades past can only wish they had so many amazing possibilities to sign up for at once.

Choosing the Perfect Place to Register

Beyond style and type of items found at any registry, there's also the important matter of choosing the perfect place to register. That is, selecting the store or site that has every advantage. That means you're looking for a registry with:

- A wide range of brand-name items, and a wide selection of choices in every area
- Affordable prices in a wide range of price points
- An easy registry process, either in-store (with scanner guns) or simple point-and-click registry features online

- Easy registry update features (such as a Delete button for items)
- The help of registry consultants, either in-store, online, or by phone
- The storage of your shipping information, cloaked for your privacy
- The store has an 800-number guests can call
- Guests who are not online can get your registry faxed to them, with the ability to fax or call their order in
- The availability of gift cards
- Gift-wrapping service
- Ease of returning gifts (such as including a gift receipt with shipped items)
- Graphics of products, with clarity of details and the ability to enlarge images
- Terrific descriptions of products, with materials and sizes easily found
- A range of color options
- Free monogramming (if applicable)
- Perks for using the registry, such as a discount on anything left on your list after the wedding (called a "completion program")
- New trends and designs of products
- An impeccable reputation in the industry
- Quick and reliable delivery of products via a certified parcel carrier
- The ability to send gifts to different addresses you specify (such as if your address changes during the time of your engagement, or directly to the shower host's home)
- Online tracking of gift delivery, so that you or your guest can check when and if the gift was delivered
- Speed of updating your registry online to reflect items as "purchased," which should take place daily or more frequently to avoid duplicate gift purchases (For instance, is it an immediate and automatic update, or will it take twenty-four hours?)

- A long gift return or exchange window, allowing you plenty of time between when the gift was purchased and when you can return it
- Incentives, such as free gifts when you register, or sweepstakes for signing on
- Excellent articles in the bridal registry section
- Helpful and friendly registry attendants in-store
- The appearance and organization of the store itself (For instance, it's a pleasure to walk the aisles, it's not organized like a warehouse store, items are easily reachable, you feel comfortable in the store itself.)
- The store has all the items you need, not just the trendiest items to the exclusion of your essentials
- Items that are not available online, and must be purchased in the store, are clearly marked on your registry
- The store provides you with either online or free printed announcement cards that can be placed in shower invitations, letting guests know where you are registered

---

How Other Couples Chose the Perfect Place

Bridal Guide's registry survey asked couples how they decided where to register. Here is what those couples said:

"They have good prices": 56.9 percent

"They have a good reputation for quality products": 56.5 percent

"Other people I know have registered there": 51.2 percent

"They are available online": 40.7 percent

"From ads or information in bridal magazines": 38.6 percent

"They have a good reputation for customer service": 21.1 percent

"My mother suggested it": 18.3 percent

"They gave me a free gift or had a sweepstakes that enticed me to register": 10.2 percent

(Survey respondents could check multiple options.)

Do You Need Some Assistance?

**According to *Bridal Guide* magazine's
registry survey . . .**

When asked if they would meet with a registry consultant to
build their lists:

"Yes, I would definitely seek the help of a registry specialist":
9.2 percent

"It would be nice, but it's not necessary": 36.1 percent

"No, we'd rather do it on our own": 54.7 percent

Many bridal registry counters and services offer the help of trained
registry consultants, who will give you pointers, identify crucial choices
for your home essentials, point you in the right direction when you
need guidance in the store, and make sure your registry choices are
being recorded correctly. Some couples love having a registry
concierge at their disposal and find their assistance truly helpful. "We
would have forgotten so many things in that store if she hadn't pointed
out our missed stops," says one engaged couple from San Antonio.

Others say they don't need or want anyone trailing them—that's
why they didn't bring their mothers or friends along. They want to
make their own choices without anyone else's input. "We started registering once, with an assistant in tow, and she was in Super Sales-
woman mode, really being too pushy about us registering for the
sickeningly expensive pots and pans. We felt too pressured, so we left
and came back on our own later."

This example points out the importance of working with the
right registry consultant, someone who's there to listen, to answer
your questions and provide gentle, unobtrusive guidance. When you
find the right assistant, you know it. When you don't, simply let the
assistant who's climbing the shelves to get you the footbath *she* thinks
you need that you've changed your minds and would like to proceed
through the rest of the registry on your own. Thank her for her help,
and tell her you'll come to the counter to deliver your registry list in
a little while. She can scan through then, and she might even catch

that you didn't register for washcloths. It's a gracious "firing" that returns the task to a more enjoyable level for you both.

Your Meeting with the Registry Consultant

It's a wise idea to make an appointment with any registry's professional consultant, getting you both started on the right foot. You'll learn the details of their registry, perhaps discover new features you didn't know existed, receive printouts and pamphlets on the store's top sellers and newest trends, and ask any questions *you* have about how the registry works.

Schedule your appointment in-person, in-store, online, or over the phone, always making sure to set up your meeting for a convenient time when you can both relax and spend plenty of time going through your registry options. So, consider whether you'd like to make this meeting for a weekday evening, when the store might be less crowded than on a Saturday or Sunday morning, or first thing in the morning on a Sunday when you're both refreshed.

When you do sit down with a consultant, be ready to explain the style and colors you want for your rooms, what you already own, what trends you're interested in trying out, and where you are as far as stocking your home—as in, are you starting from scratch or building on your existing belongings? Your meeting will be most optimal if you both have a clear idea of what you want *before* stepping into the store. Don't count on a registry consultant to create your vision or talk your partner into styles and items you want. This is purely a guidance service, there for you to enhance your registry choices according to your vision.

Who's Going with You?

When asked by *Bridal Guide* who would accompany them as they register, survey-responding brides said:

Fiancé: 89.9 percent

Mother: 16.1 percent

Friend: 12.5 percent

I will go alone: 6.9 percent

(Survey note . . . multiple answers entered by respondents.)

Chapter 8

Letting Guests Know
Where to Go

Your guests need to know where you are registered, and the old, strict rules of etiquette (which stated that you *never* put anything about gift registries on invitations) have flown out the window. Now, it's rare for a shower invitation to arrive in the mail *without* printed notice of where the bride and groom are registered, so you're in the clear. Wedding invitations, of course, still stand as being off-limits for gift registry mentions, though. On shower invitations, a simple "Registry at Macy's and Home Depot" is well accepted. Most of your guests will take it from there, either going online or in-store to check out your list.

It's on Our Site

If you decide to create your own personalized wedding Web site, you can set up links from your site directly to your registry accounts. Your guests receive the URL for your wedding Web site on your Save the Date card, and all the information they'll need is right there at the click of a mouse. A visit to your site directs them right to your registry lists. It couldn't be easier.

In addition, they'll all get to see wonderful pictures and the story of your proposal, perhaps read updates on how the wedding plans are going, "meet" the bridal party, and receive directions and links to your wedding site and their hotel options.

Visit www.wedstudio.com to see the sample Web site showing how links to the registry work. Don't have a wedding Web site? Ask for a subscription as a gift from family or friends. There's no better way to let near and faraway guests share in your pre-wedding excitement and save yourself time and energy—it's all right there on your site!

Keep in mind that some registries *give* you your own personalized wedding Web site as part of your registry with them. So, before shopping for your own site, or signing up for a free site on one of the major bridal home pages, check to see if your desired registry provides this freebie for you.

Ease of Use

Most bridal registries are created to make it easy for your guests to find your list. At most sites, they'll only have to plug in a last name (yours or his) and a state. The matching possibilities come right up on the screen. One click, and they're there.

What's great about the option of typing in either the bride's *or* the groom's last name is that some guests might not know your last name. If the guest is a distant relative of the groom, or the groom's family's work colleague, they might never have met you before. Fortunately, today's registries plan for this, so finding any couple's list has never been easier.

You *will* see, however, that some sites do give you the option of requiring a password in order for your guests to access your bridal registry. This is done purely for your privacy and security, and some couples do like knowing that their registry choices can be seen only by their invited guests, and not by any strangers, exes, stalkers, and so forth. If you do choose to join or create a password-protected registry, you can still allow your guests easy access by including the password on the printed registry cards given out with your shower invitations.

One big making-it-easier qualifier you will likely agree with is that your guests can see graphics of your gift items online, in good-quality photographs that can be enlarged if possible. Of course your guests want to see what you're asking for! Of course they want to see the details of your stemware or china patterns! According to *Bridal Guide's* survey, 55.3 percent of their brides and grooms say that it's very important that gifts can be seen on the Internet, 39.8 percent say it would be nice but it's not critical, and only 4.9 percent say it's not important—that guests will know they like it because it was their choice.

Ship It Right to You

Another noble feature of most registries is that they'll keep your shipping address on file (either displaying it on your registry or keeping it private), so that guests can very easily arrange to have their purchased registry items sent right to you. Be sure that any registry you sign up for has this option, giving all of your guests the freedom from having to look up your home address.

Again, printed registry cards are available from the registries themselves, and you can request plenty to enclose in invitations, leading your guests right to the ideal registry and the items you have chosen.

When Guests Want to Go to the Store

It might sound odd to you, savvy online shopper that you are, but some of your guests might be hesitant about shopping on the Internet. They'd rather go in person to the store where you're registered, retrieve your gift list from the registry counter, and shop the aisles themselves. They want to *see* that coffeemaker in their hands, not in a small picture on a Web site. They want to step on that bathroom scale or feel those plush towels before they buy them and wrap them up for you.

In-store purchases are reported at the registry counter and then marked as "complete" on your online registry. Don't worry about duplicates . . . so long as guests go by the rules and report your chosen gift at the registry counter. Will you get duplicates? Perhaps. But sometimes duplicates are a good thing. Extra towels, extra wine glasses . . . you can use them all.

Chapter 9

Meeting Guests' Budgets

Although it's terrific that you're signing up for the Good Stuff—high-quality bakeware, luxury bedding sets, and barbecue grills—of course it's a smart idea for you to keep your guests' budgets in mind as well. After all, if your collection of $200+ items is outside their budget limits, they'll go off-list and choose other items.

It seems I'm stating the obvious . . . not *all* of your gifts are going to be priced in the stratosphere, after all . . . but I wanted to remind you that listing a great range of options in the more moderate price bracket is likely to net you more of what you need.

The wise and gracious wedding couple does make sure to provide great midpriced gift options, items invited guests will be thrilled about giving. Guests want to give you what you need, but they also want the gift to reflect well on them to some degree. So, you'll have your wire whisk at $2.99, your spatula at $3.99, and then dozens of great $25 to $50 gifts, leading up to the higher-ticket items.

Don't forget, your guests might be carrying some heavy expenses just to attend your wedding—perhaps airfare, hotel rooms, wardrobes, tux rental if your wedding will be black tie or white tie, other gifts for your showers. Some might need to pay for babysitting. And that's just for *your* wedding! They might have six other weddings to attend that season. That's a big financial obligation on their part.

Speaking of big financial obligations, understand the mind-set of guests who have recently lost their jobs, gotten divorced, or are burdened by high medical bills. New parents might be under a cash crunch, and elderly guests might be just scraping by on a fixed income.

These loved ones aren't happy about having money issues. They want to get you a terrific wedding gift, something you truly want and need. And they know there are far wealthier guests coming to the shower and the wedding who can afford those cashmere sheets or that bistro-worthy espresso maker.

So, make life easier on them by selecting midpriced items you adore and look forward to receiving. Thank them with a written note and tell them how much you love those juice glasses—that you use every day.

"Gifts Under $25"

Need some extra inspiration for fabulous gift items in what you consider moderate price ranges? Many of the top bridal registries feature special links to their suggested "Gifts Under $25" page. Terrific items are featured with all buying information. Depending on your personal or regional idea of a "moderate price range," you could find yourself clicking on the "Gifts Under $50" or "Gifts Under $100" icons. These special pages offer you terrific additional registry ideas, so check them out.

It's not the price of the item that matters to you, after all. It's the place the item takes in your most memorable moments and daily routines.

As for those luxurious, big-ticket items you're dreaming about, you can still get those, too. Even if your guests do have cash crunch problems. Here's how . . .

Chapter 10

Group Gifts

Guests on a budget can join forces to purchase a terrific group gift. Even if guests are *not* on a budget, the group gift is a favorite.

A $500 bedding set is a terrific option for groups of work friends to chip in on.

Family members, perhaps siblings, can all go in on that $600 set of *all* the top-quality, name-brand skillets and cooking pans, completing that portion of your registry for you.

The bridesmaids can chip in to get you that $200 food processor, or the entire bridal party can contribute $50 each to get you that terrific television set, or $100 each for that plasma screen TV.

When guests join forces (and wallets), they share the satisfaction of knowing they purchased for you one of your dream items from your registry without spending a fortune individually. After all, a terrific gift belies the fact that they may have given only $30 each. You're not keeping track. You're just happy you have that mixer set or your bedding set. And they're happy to make your wish come true.

Parents can join in, as can work colleagues, golf buddies, yoga class buddies, the ladies from the book club, all your distant friends from your old hometown, your college roommates, your neighbors. Individual groups of like-minded people can band together to get you your top big-ticket item(s).

The Top Choices for Group Gifts
- Cookware sets, including fine nonstick pots, pans, and skillets
- Bakeware sets, including casserole dishes, cake dishes, and pie dishes

- A full fine china set, twelve place settings
- A full formal stemware set, twelve place settings
- Furniture, like that new queen-size bed you've wanted for years
- Luxury bedding, full sets with all accessories
- Plasma screen television sets
- Home security systems
- Subscriptions to cable services or TiVo
- Top-of-the-line power tool sets
- Patio furniture
- Swimming pool or hot tub
- Barbecue grill sets
- Chef-quality kitchen appliances
- A specially designed wine cellar with your starter collection of fine wines
- A year's worth of landscaping services
- A year's worth of personal chef service, with gourmet meals coming right to your home
- Laptop computers or other home office equipment like scanners and color copiers—they're investing in your future work success, after all
- Honeymoon elements, including hotel stay, airfare, or a lineup of activities
- Your wedding night newlywed suite at a fine hotel
- A piece of fine art from a gallery to start or enhance your collection

The group gift is a growing trend at weddings, so be sure to list items your own individual groups of friends and family can give you together. See the additional ideas under "Unique Registries" in Chapter 38 for more big-ticket inspiration.

- Professional-level golf club sets
- Membership to a golf club or country club
- A full set of camping gear, including tents and backpacks
- And yes, those mountain bikes or kayaks

Part Three

REGISTER WISELY

Chapter 11

How to Get Exactly What You Want

Now that you know the trends in registries and have perhaps discovered new areas of your home or yard that you want to register for, and now that you've given your guests' budgets some thought, it's time for the two of you to begin creating your registry game plan.

The first thing I'm going to ask you to do is create your own priorities list. Which rooms of your home do you want to focus on the most? Do you want to stock your kitchen with all the top chef-quality gear and appliances above all else? If your living room is just fine the way it is, then perhaps you'll choose to register more for that dream kitchen. Perhaps your top choice is your bedroom, decking it out in all new bedding and décor, lighting, and a romance-ready sound system.

Together, think about areas of highest priority. And keep in mind, you don't have to *agree*. You could have one room as your top focus (like the bedroom), and your groom could have another (like the backyard). That's absolutely fine. There's no one way to do this. You're creating your game plan your way, and if you have two separate top choices, then that's how you'll register.

A sample priorities list might look like this:

Our Top Registry Priorities

1. (My choice) Bedroom	6. Living room
1. (His choice) Backyard	7. Honeymoon
2. Kitchen	8. Charities
3. Dining room	9. Hi-tech items, like plasma
4. Bathrooms	TV, security system
5. Home office	10. Music and art

Now, after brainstorming and discussing for a while, record your own priorities list here, with the freedom to make several sections a number one choice:

1._____	9._____
2._____	10._____
3._____	11._____
4._____	12._____
5._____	13._____
6._____	14._____
7._____	15._____
8._____	16._____

As you explore the world of registries, you might find yourselves changing your priorities and focus around a bit. That backyard category could move up the ranks once you see fabulous portable bars and hammocks during your search. A great Fiestaware dinner set for your backyard patio could knock your bathroom accessories out of the number three spot. It's all going to be flexible. I just wanted to start you off with a basic focus plan so that you *do* register completely for the rooms you most favor in your home.

Pre-Registry Training?

Some in-store registries offer *pre-registry* courses, booklets, and even videos that give you a tour of their departments, educational tips on how to shop for china or linens, and even brand-name suggestions to add to your shopping list.

Don't Forget There Are *Four* Seasons

This has to be the one concept that so many brides and grooms in the past have forgotten . . . and then deeply regretted. Thinking only about their wedding taking place in the summer, they've forgotten to register for winter items, like a heavier down comforter or flannel sheets and throw blankets, snow shovels and winter décor items. Those bright yellow and pink summery casual dinnerware sets don't really cut it in the winter months when the season calls for deeper wine colors, hunter greens, and navies.

It can be an overwhelming distraction when you're walking through a home décor store in the spring and seeing all the gorgeous sheet sets and bedroom displays in the colors of the season. You're not thinking cold-weather fabrics like flannels and more wintry color schemes at that time. It's not right there in front of you because the store is stocked for the summer. You have to actually look beyond the displays to what you'll need later.

So, think right now about how you want your home to look and feel in both warm-weather *and* cold-weather months, and register accordingly.

"We loved the pale sage green sheets to work with our tan-colored bedroom. It was just the perfect summery look, like a suite at a resort. But then we thought that it would look a little bit 'off' in the winter. So we registered for a full set of bedding, window treatments, and additional décor to turn the room into a more burgundy look. It was just perfect for fall and winter, and it gave us the chance to have two completely different 'feels' to the room." —Audra and Carlos

Our Two Color Schemes

Spring/Summer: _____

Fall/Winter:_____

Items to "Double-Register" For

- Bedroom décor
- Blankets and comforters
- Casual dinnerware (pastels for summer, burgundies or deeper tones for winter)
- Casual drinkware (winter-themed mugs for hot chocolate in the winter vs. brightly colored margarita glasses for summer)
- Formal dinnerware
- Kitchen and bar appliances
- Living room slipcovers (lighter colors for spring and summer, then deeper, richer tones for winter)
- "Partyware"—theme-printed drink pitchers and platters for both seasons (daisies for summer, snowmen for winter)
- Pillow shams
- Robes (lighter cotton vs. heavier cotton)
- Season-appropriate outdoor tools (garden hose for summer, snow blower for winter)
- Season-appropriate outdoor "toys" (hammock for summer, car seat warmer for winter)
- Season-appropriate sporting goods (tennis racquets for summer, skis for winter)
- Sofa pillows (matching the lighter vs. deeper color scheme)
- Sofa throws
- Table linens
- Wall art
- Window treatments

Don't forget about kitchen appliances. That margarita blender could make your summer, and you might make every meal on your barbecue with those fabulous seafood baskets and rotisserie attachments, but then when the cooler weather comes, you'll be all about your slow cooker, fondue pot, and espresso maker. Look at each registry Web site's "Seasonal" section, where you'll find great shopping inspiration for all four seasons. (Would you really have thought about winter holiday décor right now?) Then load up on an even greater selection of items for your home and lifestyle.

Did You Know . . . ?

Your favorite china set just might have a holiday version, or a holiday-themed, color-coordinating serving set. When you shop for your china pattern, ask your registry coordinator or sales representative to check for you. Some china patterns actually have their own designed holiday pieces. Or your registry or sales professional can recommend an *additional* china pattern that could work as an ideal mix and match set to "winter up" your china and serving sets. (Like terrific all-black charger plates to set off the delicate gray and white in your Sweet Leilani china pattern, or a winter-colorful, patterned accent plate to place atop each dinner plate. Eight new red plates can turn your formal table settings into something more seasonal.)

The same goes for your glassware and stemware registry options. So, be sure to ask for the cold-weather versions as well.

Mix and Match

Here's another area you might miss out on (if you didn't have this book in hand!): You don't have to stick with packaged sets of china or casual dinnerware, glassware, barware, even linens. You're free to mix and match your own desired designs of everything from your place settings to your bathroom towels. Use your inner interior decorator to pair up a unique arrangement of solid-color plates and banded flatware, or mix up the fabrics for your bedroom pillows, throwing in a faux fur or a suede pillow for extra depth and luxury. Stray from the matching set of bathroom accessories and use some solids with a touch of some floral patterns in a coordinating color. Get the solid-color dinner plates with the banded-edge coffee cups and saucers. Mix the light blue sheets with the dark blue. It's your home! Accessorize as you wish!

Go Classic, and Dress It Up Later

Keep the mix-and-match concept in mind with this one. You undoubtedly know and hope that your china pattern will last you a lifetime. So, the design you choose today is going to have to suit your tastes thirty years from now. Though some couples look for the art deco design that's "them" at this moment, others choose a more classic style—like a plain porcelain with a silver band around the edge, or with a light pink floral band. Wisely, these couples who register for simpler, more classic styles of china and formal dinnerware know that they can accessorize their place settings later. They can create new looks around their classic and timeless china pattern with new, colored chargers, new salad plates in a more trendy design that works perfectly with that pink floral or silver band, new coffee cups, or a chic, trendy tablecloth that makes those classic place settings work ideally.

Register for Your Cooking Abilities?

Some bad advice is floating around implying that you should register for your current cooking level. If you're a starter chef, for instance, the advice says you should register for just the basics you'll need in your kitchen.

Nonsense!

Sure, you might be a starter chef. Boiling water might be your best talent in the kitchen. And whisks might confuse you. But that's *now*. You'll undoubtedly learn more about cooking and the culinary arts as time goes by. Perhaps together, if you sign up for cooking courses as a duo.

There's no such thing as "You're not ready for these chef's knives" in the world of wedding registries. Even starter chefs and those with little to no cooking skills find that once they register for the Good Stuff, they make more of an effort to learn how to use them. Spending more time in the kitchen together becomes even more enticing when wonderful cookware and appliances are waiting there for you to use.

Don't limit yourselves. Register for the best quality items out there, specialty cooking tools, and fun appliances, taking the time now to stock up on kitchen supplies you'll both grow to love.

Make No Mistakes

They make it so easy to scan barcodes in the stores—or point and click an item, and the SKU number is automatically entered—that it's almost impossible *not* to get the item you want on your list.

Consider this list a friendly reminder so that you'll receive *exactly* what you ask for:

1. *Pay attention to quantities.* Especially when you're registering for dishes, glasses, utensils, champagne flutes, and so on. Be extra careful that you're aware of the number of items in a set, that "1" means one glass, and not one set of eight glasses. Brides and grooms who don't focus on the numbers have found themselves registered for eight sets of eight glasses, confusing their list-shopping guests.

2. *Specify colors.* Your guests will look for this information if it's not clear in your choices of gifts. For instance, if all of the dishes and coffee mugs you register for are white, they won't be able to tell that you have a blue kitchen. Thus, the green dish towels they buy you . . . and that you'll wind up returning. In the "Notes" section of your registry, be sure to specify that your color schemes are, for instance:

- Kitchen: yellow and cream
- Bathroom: sage and cream
- Living room: chocolate and cream
- Bedroom: sage and cream
- And so on . . .

3. *Make sure monograms are specified.* For some linens and special items (like picnic blankets), you might wish to register for a particular style of monogram. Make sure the font is in the style of your choice—a pretty scroll rather than block letters, for instance—and that the letters are legible. L's can look like I's, for instance. It's a wise move to add your specified monogram font in notes to your registry where you can.

4. *Specify sizes.* Of course, you know to register for queen-size sheets if you have a queen-size bed. That's a detail to pay attention to when you're registering, especially online. But you should also be aware of the sizes of items you're selecting. If you don't look at the height

of those champagne flutes, for instance, they might not fit on the shelf where you plan to display them. Dishes might be too big or too small. Plates might not fit well in chargers. Even if you have to keep a tape measure handy to "eyeball" sizes, it's a wise pre-check to avoid returns later.

5. *Find out what "sets" consist of.* Again, this can be something you miss while registering because some Web site writeups inexplicably provide this information in small print. You should know if the bedding set contains pillowcases and a dust ruffle, for instance. You should be aware if your dinnerware set contains all of the accessories such as a gravy boat, salt and pepper shakers, and butter dish, or if each of those items are sold separately. Missing the details could mean you haven't registered for all the items you want.

6. *Check out the material.* You're reading a lot about higher thread counts meaning softer material, and that 100 percent Egyptian cotton towels are among the most luxurious out there. But how do they feel to you? Step inside the store and check them out by touch before you add any fabric items to your list. You'll be living with your sheets and towels every day for a long time to come, so be sure you get what you really want.

> *"We thought we wanted combed cotton sheets until we stopped in the store and felt the cotton jersey sheets. They were so soft, and we fell in love with them on the spot. So we switched our registry to get the new sheets. The combed cotton ones had been a suggestion from my sister, and we both felt they were just not right for us." —Jean and Sam*

7. *Check your registry.* And of course, make sure the item you register for comes up correctly on your online registry or in-store print-out. Get a copy for yourselves and be sure all is correct before you announce that your registry is up and running.

Remember, not *all* registries are done online, with a scanner gun recording item SKU numbers. In some specialty stores and independent boutiques, the registry consultants record items the old-fashioned way: by hand. So be sure to double-check his or her notes to be sure you've registered for all the right things.

How Far in Advance to Register?

The *WeddingBells* magazine and WeddingChannel.com survey says that most couples complete and announce their registries an average of 6.5 months before the wedding.

The *Bridal Guide* magazine survey says that brides and grooms are registering at the following times:

One to two months in advance: 2.8 percent

Three to four months in advance: 22.0 percent

Five to six months in advance: 40.6 percent

More than six months in advance: 34.6 percent

Store owners tell me that they're seeing brides and grooms come in to register much earlier than they have in past years, some as much as a year in advance when there are engagement parties planned in their honor.

What's Your Password?

If you plan to maintain your registry online, updating it often as most couples do, you must keep track of your password. Registries require that you password-protect your account so that no one else can get in, change your requests, eliminate items, or make any other alterations (like changing your shipping address so that all of your wedding gifts get shipped to *them*). It's all about Internet security, so keep your password safe and private.

If you do forget your password, then call the customer service number for the registry in question, or send them an e-mail, to get a reminder or help you create a brand-new password.

Chapter 12

Gift Cards

O ne absolute *must* on any bridal registry is gift cards. Lots of them.

Your guests can click on or in-store purchase gift cards in denominations from $25 to $200 in most cases, and with these valuable cards in hand, *you* get the greatest shopping trip ever. Here's why more and more brides and grooms are registering for gift cards or making a note that gift cards are welcome presents:

- It's the best shopping trip ever when both bride and groom go to the store and fill their shopping cart up with $1,000 worth of items, all pre-paid. No stress, no guilt, only pure excitement.

- You can get all the crucial items you didn't receive as shower or wedding gifts—towels, everyday dishes, juice glasses— without dipping into your wedding cash gifts or building up your credit card balances to buy yourselves the essentials.

- You can use all $1,000 worth of gift card value to buy yourselves that one big-ticket item you've been dreaming about, instead of a dozen kitchen gadgets and small appliances.

- You get to select your own stuff, which means no returning gifts you didn't like.

- If you both have different tastes, you can split up the gift cards you receive and each get the appliances, gadgets, or linens you like separately. No compromises, no arguing . . . you both get exactly what you want.

Chapter 13

Updating Your Registry

S ure, you could create your registry and then leave it alone, never
looking at it again, but why miss all the fun? Countless brides
and grooms update their registries often, adding additional items
they want to receive as gifts, even removing items they've decided
they no longer want. Those impulse clicks on those chicken-themed
potholders . . . gone. Another set of towels? Add that to the list.

According to *WeddingBells* magazine and WeddingChannel.com's
most recent survey, 51 percent of their responding brides and grooms
say they actively maintain their registries online. Most couples do,
since there's always a new inspiration, always a new segment on *Trading Spaces* that features a terrific new décor idea, always a gorgeous ad
in a magazine featuring luxurious ottomans and cashmere throws.

You don't get only one shot at creating your registry, so do yourselves a favor and update regularly.

*"We found we didn't register for enough things! After our bridal
shower, the registry was practically cleaned out. We knew that we had
a lot of guests coming for the wedding, and that they'd want gift
ideas for us, so we added more items for our living room, some more
dishware, and another set of sheets. We also tapped into some pampering items for our bathroom—spa robes, lavender bath oil sets,
candles. Once we started updating, we really loaded our list with
fabulous things we wanted."* —Leila and Tony

You might find that, as time goes by, you've forgotten to register
for a particular room: the bathroom, for instance, or a home office.
The freedom to update often during the time before your wedding
allows you that second chance to create the perfect registry list.

A Financial Advantage

Here's another reason to update your registry often . . .

Many registry programs will grant you *discounts* on any items that remain unpurchased on your registry list. Once your wedding date passes, you will then get 10 percent, 15 percent, even 20 percent or more off the items you wish to buy for yourselves later. If you're using those gift cards, this post–wedding discount could net you several *additional* items for free. Brides have been whispering this advice to each other, posting this gem of a hint on bridal message boards, and e-mailing each other about the benefits of adding more items to their lists.

Brides and Grooms Who Wish They'd Updated

"We didn't want to 'spoil the surprise' by checking in on our bridal registry list. I'm a snoop, so I know I'd be looking at it every week to see if someone got us those Calphalon pots, or if we got the DVD player. So we both promised we wouldn't even look. Big mistake! Our registry got cleaned out early, and many of our guests shopped outside of our gift choices. So we received a lot of things we didn't want as wedding gifts. We had to take them back for exchanges, and it was a big hassle." —Gina and Tom

"We were incredibly exhausted by the time we both had a day to register at the home décor store. So we pretty much rushed through the store, clicking away on items, and by the time an hour passed, we were really doing a pretty bad job of choosing everything we needed. We just weren't focused, and we forgot a lot of essential items like baking pans and a rolling pin, casual dinner plates, and an iron. Working as hard as we were, and planning the wedding, had us drained, not to mention planning a long-distance wedding, and we really never found the time to go online and add the extra things we needed. I know I wrote a note to myself to do it, but I never got around to it. So our registry was incomplete, and that made our gifts incomplete. We wound up having to use our own money to get some of the important things we needed later." —Samantha and Joshua

Chapter 14

Get Even More: Taking Advantage of Registries' Special Offers

Today's companies are smart. They know a lot of competition out there is vying for your business and there are many registries for you to consider, so they're enticing you with fabulous offers to get you even more. The best retailers offer special programs for brides and grooms—added gifts, if you will.

The discount on any remaining items on your registry list that you read about in the last chapter is just one of these new programs. The others come in variations of the following "rewards programs":

- *The referral gift.* Some registry programs offer you a special discount coupon for each additional bride- and groom-to-be whom you refer and who actually sign up for a registry.
- *The "all done" gift.* You get a discount or a gift card when your entire registry is bought out, when all of the items you registered for have been purchased.
- *Hot time gifts.* You have to be on your toes for this one, but some registries offer discounts if you update or create your registry during certain months (usually holiday months, an incentive to catch all of those holiday engagement couples).
- *Freebies.* Again, you have to be alert, because some registries offer free gifts when you sign on to register with them. It could be a crystal vase, a china picture frame, a pampering

basket, or another item they'll send you as a thank-you for choosing their store.

- *Survey gifts.* If you take the time to fill out the store's survey online, helping them collect their valuable marketing information, they'll send you a discount coupon or gift card. Some registries might even send you a "surprise gift," such as a cookbook, a photo album, or a silver pen to use with your guest book.

Always Check the Clearance Page

With your gift cards in hand, perhaps as presents you've received or those rewards gift cards you got for being a loyal customer, you can grab a bunch of bargains shopping on the store's clearance page. One bride and groom found terrific kitchen items marked down from $20 to $9.99. They were thus able to purchase more tools for their home, and they made it a habit to keep checking the Clearance link on their registry's company home page. Each month, they netted awesome bargains and got even more value from their collection of gift cards. Their motto: "We never buy anything for full price."

Chapter 15

Combining Households

You both have your own separate places and your own full sets of belongings, so it might seem to you that you already have too much stuff: his coffeemaker and your coffeemaker, his towels (green) and your towels (blue), even his bed and your bed with completely different bedding styles. Already with more belongings than you'll need for one household, why would you want to register for even *more*?

When you're combining your two households into one new home, it's most often a *different kind* of registry. Whereas many couples out there are starting completely from scratch, needing to do no more than choose the new items they want from an endless list of options, you have a few pre-steps . . . before you, too, get to select your own new gifts from that endless list of options.

Honey, That Chair Has to Go

Perhaps you have begun looking at your stuff and his stuff, discussing which items will make the move into your new house and which will make the move straight to Goodwill. You might, in fact, have already dropped huge hints about getting rid of his old ratty recliner and his threadbare rug. Out with the old and in with the new can take some serious strategizing. It could be a bigger negotiating and compromising session between the two of you than the wedding plans were. After all, it's hard to part with the familiar. It's difficult to say good-bye to things that have symbolic significance to you, and there's way too much change going on right now.

Don't get overwhelmed. It may seem like a monumental task, but you both can get through the combination process more calmly if you take it one step at a time. Use the worksheet on the following pages to organize this process of designating what you have, what you need, what stays, and what goes. This is your own individual path, since every couple is different. You might be *glad* to get rid of your old sofa. Your groom might be only too happy to finally unload that old recliner and trade in those rugs for Persian area carpets. This process could be a snap for you, made even easier by the organizational steps outlined here, or this could take a while as you both wheel and deal your "trades" and fight for your bedroom comforter with everything you have.

Make It Even Easier

Flip to the upcoming chapters in this book for complete lists of items in every category of your home (bedroom, kitchen, home office, and so on). You'll need these lists later for your official registry process, but for now you can photocopy and use them for *this* step as you create an inventory of what you already have, what you're willing to toss, what you want to upgrade, and what you need new. Highlighter pen codes work well with, say, pink denoting your keepers, blue denoting his, yellows are things you need, and greens are items for upgrade. Create your own system for inspiration and organization. We've provided two modes for you here, so that you can work together to build your list.

- *Step 1:* In with the new. This is the easy part. Just list everything you don't already have, all those fun "toys" like the DVD player, the formal dinnerware set, the picnic basket and blanket, the espresso machine, the juicer, the oversized ottomans, and so on. The moment you're done with this first list, your registry has started to take form.
- *Step 2:* It has to go. Next on the worksheet or using the upcoming checklists, you'll mark down all of your current belongings that you'll discard and replace with newer models. That means the threadbare rug and ratty recliner mentioned earlier, and it could mean your bedding sets, your dishes, your

coffee mugs, and so on. The items you both agree have had their day, and now you want the new ones. You'll then know to add these new models to your registry.

Hand-Me-Downs

Earlier in the book, you read about where to donate your discarded items, those dishes and mugs and bowls and furniture you plan to upgrade or replace. Check that section out for a reminder on places that accept your castoffs, and don't forget that family and friends just starting out might *love* your old cereal bowls, or they might want to do a little remodeling work on that recliner. It's something to keep in mind before you plan a garage sale.

Now for the More Complicated Part

When you start scouting and sifting between household items you both own, in order to decide whose spatula set you'll keep, for instance, here's where the primate territorial impulse can kick in. Some choices will, of course, be easy. You'll keep your new designer bedding. He agrees. No argument. Case closed. But other items could come to a heated discussion.

Here's your rescue . . .

If you're absolutely at an impasse and you both want to keep your own separate skillets, then keep them both. Store one in the kitchen as the everyday model, and the other in the pantry or on a higher shelf as the secondary. Box up his perfectly okay casual dinnerware set and keep it in the basement for parties at your place when you'll need additional dishes. Not everything needs to be tossed away, and not everything needs to come down to "one or the other." Decide now which items will be your secondaries and mark them on the chart.

"We loved the idea of designating some items as secondaries. It kept us from fighting right now, got those glasses into a storage box, and once he realized we never used them now that we had the good new ones, he was more agreeable about donating them to a women's shelter that could use them. The stall worked wonders." —Maya, married four years

Storage for All Your Stuff

This brings up a very important bridal registry category, more important for couples who are blending and combining their two households into one: storage and organizational systems. If you're among the couples who are merging places and belongings, you, too, will definitely want to register for plenty of storage items:

- CD and DVD organizer racks
- Closet organizing systems—several, for bedrooms, kitchens, living rooms, home offices, and basements
- Kitchen organizers like utensil storage systems, food storage containers, shelf racks that keep all your storage boxes standing on end, organized by size
- Multi-level bookshelves
- Organizing boxes and bins, like shoe boxes and under-bed flat storage boxes
- Storage ottomans, with padded tops that lift off to create handy and invisible storage space within
- Various decorative baskets and boxes, such as graphic storage boxes for photos

Check out the storage and organizer sections of your chosen registries, home décor stores, and home remodeling stores. This could be your most valuable category when it comes to creating a home that's a visual joy and a functional space.

Making His Stuff and Your Stuff Work Together

Once you have your final list of keepers in hand, and you've arranged how you'll combine your existing belongings together in your new home, here's where registering becomes rewarding and fun. You can register for items that will make "his stuff" and "your stuff" work even better together. Consider it a "sewing together" of both of your styles. You'll place items and weave color schemes together so that every item you both treasure works to create an idyllic room. Here are some examples:

- You have a hot pink sofa, he has a beige reading chair. To create your unified beige-based room, cover that hot pink sofa with a beige slipcover, and arrange those pink candles you love into attractive accents around the room.
- He has a light wood entertainment center, and your pictures are set in black lacquer frames. Register for new light wood frames, move your pictures into those, and then hang them beautifully above the entertainment center.

You get the picture. Spend plenty of time going through your belongings for each room of the house with an eye toward the new items that can "sew" together a unified décor scheme. Take your time. This is a job worth mulling over. Do one room a day if that works best for your attention spans and busy schedules. The better you invest your attention in this important job, the easier it is to register for just the right items.

This shouldn't be a painful procedure. Remember, you can always keep some items as seconds, and you may find a way—as the stories below illustrate—to turn this process into a much easier method than expected.

"We couldn't decide between his bedding set and mine, so we compromised. Looking at all our duplicates, he came up with the idea to turn our extra room into a guest bedroom rather than a storage room. So we easily decided that his bedding set and bedroom accessories would be perfect to outfit that bedroom, while mine would be ideal for our master bedroom. We registered for additional items to complete both rooms." —Colleen and Thom

"Once we got into the selection process, I was actually happy to get rid of most of my old, mismatched, hand-me-down stuff. His décor is more modern, very stylish, and I was always more comfortable at

his place than at my own. So, it was much easier for me to pick and choose from my own belongings to see where my 'touches' would accent each room. My candles, my collection of Japanese sake cups, my pictures . . . we got great shelving units to display them all, and it was a really fun rainy afternoon we spent together piecing the puzzle in place. Now, with the house all together, with my stuff blended into his stuff, it really feels like everything is Ours." —Jaclyn and Matt

"We just did a big re-shuffle of where things went. We took my French country furniture and did the living room with it, and his more modern pieces that used to be in his living room created the ideal setup for our downstairs den. Once we gave each room its own theme, we were able to move a lot of our stuff into different areas, and it all worked well together once we brought in new area rugs, new table linens, new décor. We registered for a lot of 'pull it together' pieces that made each room complete." —Paula and Warren

The Top Items for Combining Two Sets of Belongings into One Unified Home

- Sofa and chair slipcovers
- Area rugs
- Picture frames
- Décor items: pillar candles and candle trays
- Sofa pillows in coordinating colors
- Colorful throws
- Display shelving units
- Ottomans
- Organizer sets
- Framed prints and artwork
- Mirrors
- Table linens
- Room paints and wallpaper borders
- Window treatments: shades, blinds, and curtains
- Coffee tables: low and plain

Of course, you can get terrific inspiration by watching your favorite home redecorating show on television or by picking up interior decorating magazines and home décor catalogs. Consider this your chance to play artist with your home.

One final story:

"Since we already owned enough of the essentials, weaving our home together meant that we could register for the really fun, unique stuff like artwork and sculptures, candles and throws, bar sets and outdoor furniture. It gave us the chance to indulge in items we wouldn't otherwise have." —Sarah and Miguel

The His/Hers/Ours List of What Stays, What Goes, What's Needed

Item	She Has	He Has	We Need	Must GO

Item	She Has	He Has	We Need	Must GO

Part Four

MAKING YOUR SELECTIONS

Now that you know the biggest registry trends, smart tips for registering well, and perhaps even some inspiration for new areas to register for, it's time to start checking off your wish list right here. The following chapters suggest the many registry items you'll find on the market, and I encourage you to write in your own unique ideas as well.

Before we begin, let me share with you *WeddingBells* magazine and WeddingChannel.com's most recent registry survey results, so that you can see what other brides- and grooms-to-be are very excitedly adding to their own lists:

The Most Popular Types of Gifts
Cookware: 85 percent
Linens: 84 percent
Small kitchen appliances: 80 percent
Dinnerware/china: 79 percent
Vacuum: 78 percent
Crystal/stemware: 70 percent
Camera/camcorder: 57 percent
DVD player: 47 percent
Microwave: 40 percent

> **That's Billion with a "B"**
>
> Across the country, a staggering $11.9 billion is spent on registry items.

The Most Popular Type of Tableware
Dinnerware/china for casual entertaining: 41 percent
Mostly formal dinnerware and fine china: 11 percent
A mix of both styles: 48 percent

The Most Luxurious Items
China/tableware: 28 percent
Bedding: 20 percent
Cookware: 8 percent

The results of the survey showed an incredibly wide range of luxury items from honeymoons to bedroom furniture sets, cashmere sheets, KitchenAid stand mixers, and plasma TVs. The majority of respondents returned the above top choices.

Whose Idea Was It to Register for the Luxury Item?
Both bride and groom: 49 percent
Bride: 38 percent
Groom: 11 percent
Other: 2 percent

Did You Receive the Luxury Item as a Gift?
Yes: 64 percent
No: 36 percent

What Price Range Did Your Most Expensive Gift Fall Into?
Under $100: 5 percent
$100–$199:18 percent
$200–$299: 27 percent
$300–$399: 22 percent
$400–$499: 9 percent
$500–$999: 12 percent
$1,000–$2,499: 4 percent
Over $2,500: 2 percent

Of survey respondents, 72 percent received three-quarters or more of what they registered for and 75 percent purchased some if not all of the remaining items on their lists. The most expensive item from the registry was purchased by:

Family (*excluding* parents): 42 percent
Parents of bride or groom: 23 percent
Individual friends: 21 percent
Group of friends: 19 percent

The Top Items from the Hot New Registry Categories
Electronics and home entertainment: 55 percent
Home renovation: 40 percent
Lawn and garden: 35 percent
Honeymoon: 18 percent
Sporting equipment: 18 percent
Computer equipment: 3 percent

Chapter 16

Dinnerware

How many settings should you register for? Plan for at least twelve place settings if you plan to entertain in your home, or eight place settings if you foresee more casual and intimate group gatherings. The more, the better, as it's easier now to complete a larger set. Keep in mind that dinnerware and flatware sets sometimes get discontinued by their manufacturers to make room for the newest designs and trends, so your cherished set could be more difficult, and more expensive, to expand in the future.

Insider Information

Although it is considered a trade magazine and a Web site, geared toward store owners who are exploring the new hot names in tableware to stock in their shops, I suggest that you take a look through *Tableware Today* (www.tablewaretoday.com). This source gives great insider information on types of tableware, brand names, design styles, hot new tableware designers, company innovations, and new trends to give you inspiration for your own tableware choices.

This company also provides an in-depth survey of the most popular china, crystal, and flatware chosen for couples' wedding registries nationwide, which you can find on their site in each year's June/July issue. See if your own choices have made the list from the latest survey, generously provided here by *Tableware Today*:

Tableware Today polled over 100 department stores' bridal directors and specialty store owners to survey the top pattern preferences of more than 200,000 engaged couples. Here are the top picks from their survey, including "trending up" choices that have moved quickly into favored positions:

Fine Dinnerware

1. Crestwood Platinum . . . Noritake
2. Federal Platinum . . . Lenox
3. Opal Innocence . . . Lenox
4. Sweet Leilani . . . Noritake
5. Palatial Platinum . . . Mikasa
6. Pearl Innocence . . . Lenox
7. Eternal . . . Lenox
8. Solitaire . . . Lenox
9. Silver Palace . . . Noritake
10. Stoneleigh . . . Noritake

Trending Up

A. Platinum Crown . . . Mikasa
B. Grosgrain . . . Wedgwood

Casual Upstairs Dining

1. Colorwave . . . Noritake
2. Italian Countryside . . . Mikasa
3. Butterfly Meadow . . . Lenox
4. Butler's Pantry . . . Lenox
5. Energy . . . Denby
6. Garden Harvest . . . Mikasa
7. Naturewood . . . Pfaltzgraff
8. French Countryside . . . Mikasa
9. Storm . . . Denby
10. Jamberry . . . Pfaltzgraff

Trending Up

A. Blue Jetty . . . Denby
B. Swedish Lodge . . . Lenox
C. Pistoulet . . . Pfaltzgraff

Housewares Dinnerware

1. Fiesta . . . Homer Laughlin
2. Cappuccino . . . Pfaltzgraff
3. Ocean Breeze . . . Pfaltzgraff
4. Nova . . . Sango
5. Summer Breeze . . . Pfaltzgraff
6. Sphere . . . Pfaltzgraff
7. Mystic . . . Pfaltzgraff
8. French Quarter . . . Pfaltzgraff
9. Espana . . . Tabletops Unlimited
10. Arctic . . . Pfaltzgraff

Trending Up

A. Sierra . . . Pfaltzgraff
B. Sorrento . . . Signature Housewares

Specialty Store Dinnerware

1. Louvre . . . Bernardaud
2. Symphony . . . Haviland
3. Sterling . . . Wedgwood
4. Allee Royale . . . Raynaud
5. Duke of Gloucester . . . Mottahedeh

As far as finding your ideal dinnerware sets, you should know that *Bridal Guide* magazine polled their readers to find out just how they plan to find theirs.

- Engaged couples in the survey who said they would look online for pattern and style ideas: 49.8 percent
- Couples who will register for casual dinnerware: 59.2 percent
- Couples who said they were going after fine china dinnerware: 52.4 percent

Formal Dinnerware

Registered at: _____

Web site: _____

Item	Pattern Name	Quantity Desired	Registered For	Received
Bread and butter plate				
Cappuccino cups				
Cappuccino saucers				
Charger				
Coffee cup				
Demitasse set				
Dessert plate				
Dinner plate				
Espresso cups				
Espresso saucers				
Salad plate				
Saucer				
Soup bowl				
Other				
Other				
Other				
Other				
Other				
Other				
Other				
Other				
Other				

Formalware Serving Set

Registered at: _____

Web site: _____

Item	Pattern Name	Quantity Desired	Registered For	Received
Butter dish				
Cake plate				
Candlesticks				
Chafing dish				
Cheese board				
Coffee pot				
Compote				
Covered casserole dish				
Covered vegetable dish				
Creamer				
Fruit bowl				
Gravy boat				
Open vegetable dish				
Platter				
Quiche dish				
Salad bowl				
Salt and pepper shaker set				
Service/buffet dish				
Serving tray				
Silver tea serving set				
Soufflé dish				

Item	Pattern Name	Quantity Desired	Registered For	Received
Soup tureen set				
Sugar bowl				
Teapot				
Trivet				
Other				
Other				
Other				

Casual Dinnerware Set

Registered at: _____

Web site: _____

Item	Pattern Name	Quantity Desired	Registered For	Received
Five-piece place setting				
Bread and butter plate				
Dessert plate				
Dinner plate				
Salad plate				
Soup bowl				
Cappuccino cups				
Cappuccino saucers				
Cereal bowl				
Coffee mugs				
Demitasse set				
Dessert bowl				

Item	Pattern Name	Quantity Desired	Registered For	Received
Espresso cup set				
Pasta bowl				
Saucers				
Teacups				
Other				
Other				

Casual Dining Serveware

Registered at: _____

Web site: _____

Item	Pattern Name	Quantity Desired	Registered For	Received
Butter dish				
Cake plate				
Candlesticks				
Chafing dish				
Cheese board				
Coffee mugs				
Coffeepot				
Compote				
Covered casserole dish				
Covered vegetable dish				
Creamer set				
Crescent platter				
Dessert bowl				
Divided platter				

Item	Pattern Name	Quantity Desired	Registered For	Received
Fish platter				
Fondue set				
Fruit bowl				
General serving platter				
Gravy boat				
Lazy Susan				
Outdoor dining dish set				
Outdoor dining serving set				
Quiche dish				
Rectangular tray				
Salad bowl				
Salt and pepper shaker set				
Saucers				
Serving bowl				
Serving tray				
Snack dish				
Soufflé dish				
Soup tureen				
Sugar bowl				
Sushi dish set				
Teacups				
Teapot				
Thermal carafe				
Other				
Other				

Chapter 17

Flatware

Choose your model carefully, always looking for quality in a brand name with a long history. Know that silver tarnishes and requires some care in the future (polishing silver is *not* on most couples' wish list for pre-holiday prep work), so look at the shine and weight of the metals you choose, select classic designs that will last through the decades, and register for plenty of sets to allow you easy entertaining in the future.

One tip: Some formal flatware sets, when chosen in a classic design, work well as your *only* set. So, see if you need to choose a formal pattern and a casual pattern. One choice could work well for both situations.

Bridal Guide magazine's 2004 gift registry survey reveals the following about flatware choices among today's couples:

Item	Have	Registering For	We'll Buy It Ourselves
Silver-plated flatware	12.8%	48.0%	8.4%
Stainless steel flatware	23.2%	51.2%	8.0%
Sterling silver flatware	15.0%	56.0%	7.2%

The Top Flatware Designs

According to the *Tableware Today* annual bridal registry survey, which they're generously allowing me to share with you here, and which you can find online at their site www.tablewaretoday.com in the June/July 2004 issue, here are the top flatware designs on the lists of over 200,000 brides and grooms:

Stainless

1. Eternal . . . Lenox
2. Aquarius . . . Oneida
3. Classico Satin . . . Mikasa
4. Federal Platinum . . . Lenox
5. Frost . . . Oneida
6. Easton . . . Oneida
7. Studio . . . Gorham
8. Julliard . . . Oneida
9. Column . . . Gorham
10. Dover . . . Oneida

Trending Up

A. Astragal . . . Oneida
B. Capello . . . Oneida

Sterling

1. Grande Baroque . . . Wallace
2. Chantilly . . . Gorham
3. Old Master . . . Towle
4. Francis I . . . Reed and Barton
5. Joan of Arc . . . International
6. Fairfax . . . Gorham
7. Queen Elizabeth I . . . Towle
8. Rose Point . . . Wallace
9. 18th Century . . . Reed and Barton
10. Eloquence . . . Lunt

Formal Flatware Set

Registered at: _____

Web site: _____

Item	Pattern Name	Quantity Desired	Registered For	Received
Butter knife				
Cocktail fork				
Cream soup spoon				
Demitasse spoon				
Dessert spoon				
Dessert fork				
Dinner fork				
Fish fork				
Fish knife				
Iced beverage spoon				
Place spoon				
Salad fork				
Silver storage chest				
Soup spoon				
Table spoon				
Other				
Other				
Other				
Other				
Other				
Other				

Formal Serving Flatware

Registered at: _____

Web site: _____

Item	Pattern Name	Quantity Desired	Registered For	Received
Hostess set				
Serving set				
Bread knife				
Butter knife				
Cake knife				
Cheese knife				
Flat server				
Gravy ladle				
Olive fork				
Pickle fork				
Pie server				
Pierced serving spoon				
Salad serving spoons				
Serving spoon				
Soup ladle				
Sugar spoon				
Other				
Other				
Other				
Other				
Other				
Other				
Other				

Casual Flatware

Registered at: _____

Web site: _____

Item	Pattern Name	Quantity Desired	Registered For	Received
Five-piece place setting				
Dessert spoon				
Dinner fork				
Salad fork				
Soup spoon				
Teaspoon				
Serving set				
Cake knife				
Pie server				
Serving fork				
Slotted spoon				
Soup ladle				
Other				
Other				

Cutlery Sets

This is a big category, with more and more couples looking for a durable, dependable brand name, as well as chef-quality knife sets. Attractive butcher block sets are a top choice on many registries, allowing you to set out your impressive cutlery set on your well-stocked kitchen's counter.

Bridal Guide's most recent registry survey shows just how big a category this is for brides and grooms.

Item	Have It	Registered for It	We'll Buy It Ourselves
Cutlery	23.2%	52.6%	7.6%

Cutlery Sets

Registered at: _____

Web site: _____

Item	Manufacturer Name	Quantity Desired	Registered For	Received
Boning knife				
Bread knife				
Butcher block knife set				
Carving knife				
Chef's knife				
Cleaver				
Cutting board				
Kitchen shears				
Knife block				
Paring knife				
Serrated knife				
Sharpening steel set				
Slicing knife				
Steak knife set				
Tomato knife				
Utility knife				
Other				
Other				
Other				
Other				
Other				
Other				
Other				

Chapter 18

Drinkware

Let's start off formally again with your crystal stemware and then move into your everyday glasses and barware for party drinks . . .
Register for plenty of stemware and glasses—twelve is the recommended amount for registries, as again some patterns can be discontinued and hard to match in the future.

Again, *Bridal Guide*'s survey says that crystal stemware is a popular choice, with 61.6 percent of couples registering for their collections, and only 6.8 percent of couples buying their own. The survey reveals that 8.8 percent are sticking with crystal stemware they already own, perhaps an inherited set or a set from a previous marriage.

Tableware Today's Survey Results for Stemware

The site collected registry statistics for over 200,000 engaged couples' picks, compiling a master list of the most popular choices out there today. Visit www.tablewaretoday.com and look at their annual bridal survey results in their June/July 2004 issues. Here, by the generous permission of *Tableware Today* . . .

The Top Stemware Design Choices

1. Lismore . . . Waterford
2. Durand . . . Longchamps
3. Stephanie . . . Mikasa
4. Flame d'Amore . . . Mikasa
5. Debut . . . Lenox
6. Arctic Lights . . . Mikasa

(continued on next page)

---

7. Lady Annie . . . Gorham
8. French Countryside . . . Mikasa
9. Encore . . . Lenox
10. Park Lane . . . Mikasa

Trending Up

A. Vendome Platinum . . . Noritake
B. Panache . . . Mikasa

Formal Stemware

Registered at: _____

Web site: _____

Item	Pattern Name	Quantity Desired	Registered For	Received
Balloon/red wine glass				
Brandy snifter				
Champagne flute				
Cordial				
Martini				
Oversized goblet				
Water goblet				
White wine glass				
Other				
Other				
Other				

Everyday Glasses and Barware

It's not the fine crystal, but these sets of everyday glasses will be in your hands most often. They're also the glasses you'll hand out to your friends during your parties, dinners, and celebrations at your house. So invest your time well in selecting a terrific design you'll enjoy every day.

Check out the following statistics from *Bridal Guide* magazine's 2004 survey to see where other couples stack up with their drinkware and barware choices.

Item	Have It	Registered for It	We'll Buy It Ourselves
Casual glassware/ stemware	30.8%	57.2%	8.0%
Barware and accessories	9.2%	56.8%	10.4%

Everyday Glasses and Barware

Registered at: _____

Web site: _____

Item	Pattern Name	Quantity Desired	Registered For	Received
Ashtrays				
Ashtrays, cigar width				
Bar caddy set with tongs				
Beer mug				
Beermaking kit				
Coasters				
Cooler glass				

Item	Pattern Name	Quantity Desired	Registered For	Received
Double old-fashioned glass				
Glass rimmer				
Glass water or drink pitcher				
High ball glass				
Ice bucket				
Ice scoop				
Ice tongs				
Juice glass				
Margarita glass				
Martini glass				
Outdoor acrylic water or drink pitcher				
Outdoor glass sets (martini, iced tea, margarita, etc.)				
Pilsner glass				
Red wine glass				
Strainer				
Tilt cordials				
Vented pourers				
White wine glass				
Wine charms				
Wine chiller				
Wine sealer				
Wine thermometer				
Wine vacuum sealer				

Item	Pattern Name	Quantity Desired	Registered For	Received
Winemaking kit				
Other				
Other				
Other				

Bar Set

Registered at: _____

Web site: _____

Item	Pattern Name	Quantity Desired	Registered For	Received
Bar tools				
Bottle opener				
Champagne bucket				
Coasters				
Cocktail napkins				
Cocktail picks				
Cocktail shaker				
Corkscrew				
Cutting board				
Decanter				
Drink stirrers				
Drink strainer				
Ice bucket and tongs				
Irish coffee mugs				

Item	Pattern Name	Quantity Desired	Registered For	Received
Jiggers				
Juice squeezer				
Paring knife				
Pitcher				
Serving tray				
Shot glass				
Stein				
Wine charms				
Wine cooler				
Wine rack				
Wine saver				
Wine tub				
Other				
Other				
Other				
Other				
Other				
Other				

Chapter 19

Bakeware and Cookware

M ore than 80 percent of brides and grooms are searching for the perfect bakeware collections for their kitchens. Sure, these durable, nonstick pots and pans are pricey, but it's worth every penny to have the Good Stuff. These are the items you'll use most in your kitchen, and you will likely use these for many years to come, so create your ideal collection now.

Bakeware and Cookware

Registered at: _____

Web site: _____

Item	Brand Name/Style	Quantity Desired	Registered For	Received
Baking pan, round (Hint: get two or more for large batches)				
Baking pan, square				
Bundt cake pan				
Cake decorating kit				
Casserole, large				
Casserole, medium				

Item	Brand Name/Style	Quantity Desired	Registered For	Received
Casserole, small				
Cookie cutters				
Cookie dough shooter				
Double boiler				
Dutch oven				
Egg poaching pan				
Fondue set				
Fry pan, large				
Fry pan, small				
Griddle				
Grill pan				
Jelly roll				
Lasagna pan				
Lid holder				
Loaf pan				
Muffin pan				
Omelet pan, large				
Omelet pan, small				
Pasta cooker				
Pie pan				
Pizza stone or pan				
Pot rack				
Pyrex dish set				
Quiche pan				
Roasting pan, large				

Item	Brand Name/Style	Quantity Desired	Registered For	Received
Roasting pan, medium				
Roasting rack				
Sauce pan, large				
Sauce pan, medium				
Sauce pan, small				
Sauté pan, large				
Sauté pan, medium				
Sauté pan, small				
Soufflé pan				
Springform pan				
Steamer and insert				
Storage containers				
Tart pan				
Tea kettle				
Wok/stir-fry pan				
Other				
Other				

Prized Heirlooms?

Believe it or not, your baking pans could someday be handed down to your *grandchildren*, who will use them with memories of you in their hearts. So many cooks out there say that their mothers' or grandmothers' lasagna pans or cooking pots are prized possessions. And not to leave out fathers and grandfathers . . . it could be *Dad's* kitchen memories and bakeware sets that are held so dear.

Chapter 20

Kitchen Appliances

This might be your first stop when registering for your wedding gifts. After all, the blender, toaster, and coffeemaker you choose will be focal points in your kitchen, the items you use the most, the ones that start off your every day. Not to mention it's a blast seeing all the new colors and sleek designs on the market today, as well as the new added features that help these appliances make your life easier (for example, the coffeemaker that grinds the beans first).

This section begins with small kitchen appliances, then moves into larger kitchen appliances that more and more couples are signing onto their lists. Sure, a new Viking stove is expensive, but that could be a terrific group gift from your entire bridal party (and your parents too . . . and the neighbors). Nothing is off the charts for bridal registries today, so large appliances are making their way onto a greater number of registries. You'll need these big appliances, too, especially if you plan to renovate your home after the wedding.

Bridal Guide magazine reports in with their 2004 survey on which small kitchen appliances top the shopping lists of today's brides and grooms.			
Item	Have It	Registered for It	We'll Buy It Ourselves
Blender	41.2%	50.8%	4.8%
Breadmaker	11.2%	46.4%	14.4%
Can opener	49.6%	36.4%	5.6%

Item	Have It	Registered for It	We'll Buy It Ourselves
Cappuccino/ espresso maker	10.4%	39.2%	13.6%
Coffee maker	36.0%	42.0%	7.6%
Food processor	15.2%	53.6%	8.8%
Handheld mixer	41.6%	49.2%	4.4%
Indoor grill	28.0%	32.8%	12.4%
Juicer	11.6%	41.2%	11.6%
Microwave	60.4%	24.8%	6.4%
Pressure cooker	12.4%	45.2%	10.4%
Slow cooker	35.6%	39.2%	9.6%
Stand mixer	13.2%	60.4%	8.8%
Waffle maker	19.2%	46.0%	10.0%

Small Appliances

Registered at: _____

Web site: _____

Item	Brand Name/ Model	Color	Quantity Desired	Registered For	Received
Blender					
Bread machine					
Breadmaker					
Cappuccino maker					
Coffee grinder					
Coffeemaker					
Convection oven					

Item	Brand Name/ Model	Color	Quantity Desired	Registered For	Received
Drink mixer					
Electric buffet					
Electric can opener					
Electric carving knife					
Electric deep fryer					
Electric skillet					
Electric crepe maker					
Electric wok					
Espresso maker					
Fondue set					
Food processor					
Food vacuum sealer set					
French coffee press					
Frozen yogurt maker					
Hand blender					
Hand mixer					
Ice cream maker					
Ice shaver					
Indoor grill					
Juicer					
Knife sharpener					
Meat slicer					
Microwave oven					
Mini chopper					

Item	Brand Name/ Model	Color	Quantity Desired	Registered For	Received
Panini machine					
Pasta maker					
Pizzelle maker					
Popcorn maker					
Pressure cooker					
Quesadilla maker					
Rice cooker					
Rotisserie oven					
S'mores maker					
Sandwich grill					
Slow cooker					
Standup mixer					
Steamer					
Tea maker (hot and iced model)					
Toaster, bagel					
Toaster, standard					
Toaster oven with broiler					
Tortilla maker					
Waffle maker, Belgian					
Waffle maker, hearts					
Waffle maker, standard					
Wine chiller					
Other					
Other					

Large Appliances

Registered at: _____

Web site: _____

Item	Brand Name/ Model	Color	Quantity Desired	Registered For	Received
Air conditioner					
Deep freezer					
Dishwasher					
Dryer					
Heating unit					
Refrigerator					
Stove					
Washing machine					
Wine refrigerator					
Other					
Other					
Other					
Other					
Other					

Chapter 21

Kitchen Gadgets

The top kitchen gadgets on many registries continue to be the basics—measuring spoons, spatulas, measuring cups—but there's a big growth in unique gadgets, specialty items for all the great dishes you'll make and the creative ways you'll serve them . . .

According to *Bridal Guide* magazine's latest registry survey, 31.2 percent of couples say they already have their kitchen gadget collections, 63.2 percent have registered for them, and only 4.4 percent plan to spend their own money to buy them.

Kitchen Gadgets

Registered at: _____

Web site: _____

Item	Brand Name	Quantity Desired	Registered For	Received
Apple corer/ slicer				
Avocado slicer				
Bag sealer				
Baking rack				
Basting brush				

Item	Brand Name	Quantity Desired	Registered For	Received
Bottle brush				
Bottle opener				
Canister set				
Canning jars				
Can opener				
Cheese grater				
Cheese knife				
Cheese plane				
Cheese slicer				
Cherry pitter				
Chip bag clips				
Chocolate thermometer				
Citrus reamer				
Cleaning brushes				
Clock				
Coasters				
Colander				
Cookie dough scoop				
Corncob holders				
Cutting boards				
Dish towels				
Dough cutter				
Egg separator				
Food scale				
Food storage containers				
Fruit brushes				

Item	Brand Name	Quantity Desired	Registered For	Received
Funnel set				
Garlic press				
Hand chopper				
Ice cream scoop, heated				
Ice cream scoop, regular				
Ice cube trays				
Jar opener				
Julienne peeler				
Kitchen timer				
Ladles				
Lemon zester				
Measuring cups (chefs say, "Get several!")				
Measuring spoons				
Meat tenderizer				
Meat thermometer				
Microwave plate covers				
Milk frother				
Mixing bowls				
Napkin holder				
Nutcracking set				
Oven mitt set				
Paper towel holder				
Parer				

Item	Brand Name	Quantity Desired	Registered For	Received
Pasta fork				
Pasta press				
Pastry bag				
Pastry bag accessories				
Pastry brush				
Pizza cutter				
Potato masher				
Potato ricer				
Recipe holder				
Rolling pin				
Salad spinner				
Salt and pepper mill				
Scrubbers				
Seafood cracking set				
Seafood picks				
Serving spoon				
Shish kebab holders				
Sifter				
Slotted spoon				
Soda can dispenser rack				
Spatula set				
Spice rack				
Splatter screen				
Spoon rest				
Strainers				

Item	Brand Name	Quantity Desired	Registered For	Received
Strawberry huller				
Table sweeper				
Thermometer				
Tongs				
Toothpick dispenser				
Tortilla warmer				
Trivets				
Utensil jar or pitcher				
Vegetable peeler				
Vented pourer				
Water filter system				
Wire whisks				
Wooden spoons				
Other				
Other				
Other				
Other				
Other				
Other				
Other				
Other				
Other				
Other				
Other				
Other				

Chapter 22

Home Décor Accessories

D on't forget to add stylish accents to your home, those touches of color and focal points that can combine your belongings seamlessly.

Accessories

Registered at: _____

Web site: _____

Item	Design/Color/ Brand Name	Quantity Desired	Registered For	Received
Aquarium				
Aquarium accessories				
Area rugs				
Book collection (leather-bound, first edition, sets, etc.)				
Bookends				
Candelabra				
Candleholders				
Carpeting				
CD rack				

Item	Design/Color/ Brand Name	Quantity Desired	Registered For	Received
Ceiling fan accessories				
Ceiling fans				
Chandelier				
Decorative lampshades for existing lamp				
Decorative throw pillows				
Display shelving units				
DVD rack				
Faux plants and flowers				
Finials for window treatments				
Fireplace candle-holder rack				
Fireplace screen				
Fireplace tool set				
Flooring kit, hardwood floor				
Flooring kit, laminate				
Flooring kit, tile				
Frame artwork				
Hearth rug				
Holiday decorations				
Holiday ornaments				
Lamp, floor				
Lamp, table				

Item	Design/Color/ Brand Name	Quantity Desired	Registered For	Received
Lighting systems, art or décor pinlights				
Lighting systems, dimmer switches				
Lighting systems, outdoor/ backyard/ pool accents				
Lighting systems, recessed lighting				
Lighting systems, track lighting				
Live plants and potted flowers				
Magazine rack				
Mirrors				
Photo albums				
Photo storage boxes				
Picture frames, tabletop				
Picture frames, wall mounted				
Pillar candles				
Plant holder stands				
Portable waterfall fountains				
Room dividers				
Sculptures				
Snack trays				
Stencil supplies				

Item	Design/Color/ Brand Name	Quantity Desired	Registered For	Received
Throw blankets				
Umbrella stand				
Vases (get plenty!)				
VHS rack				
Votive candle sets				
Wallpaper borders				
Welcome mats				
Wine rack				
Other				
Other				
Other				
Other				
Other				

Cool Selection

Flooring is a growing category for the home decorating couple. Now, you can register for boxed kits containing either hardwood floor materials that snap together, tile kits with cutters, even laminate flooring that you'll use to put a new finish underfoot.

Transforming a room into one with hardwood floors is a thrill when you see the finished product, and it also may add value to your home. So, consider joining the ranks of brides and grooms who are signing up for flooring materials . . . including—get this—underfloor heating systems. No more cold kitchen floors in the morning.

Chapter 23

Linens

D on't look for pillowcases and duvet covers here. I cover linens
for your bedroom in chapter 28, giving those luxury sheet
sets their own special, separate treatment.

This section is reserved for your living room and dining room
linens, table and sofa varieties.

According to *Bridal Guide* . . .

The magazine's latest survey reveals that when it comes
to table linens, 14.8 percent of engaged couples
already own their sets, a whopping 72 percent have
registered for them, and only 10 percent plan to buy
their own.

As you've read, the trend in bridal registries is for luxury fabrics:
100 percent Egyptian cotton, cashmere, even leather-lined fabrics for
sofa slipcovers and some curtains. The fabric industry is alive and
well, not just in haute couture fashion but in fashion for your home.
Learn all you can about the quality and care of your favorite fabrics—both luxury styles and down-home varieties like jersey fabrics
and cool cottons, chenille and laces—and take the touch test in-store
before you add to your registry.

Know Your Size

Be sure to measure your tabletops and indicate whether you want oval, round, square, or rectangular tablecloths. As with your wedding dress, the size you choose needs to fit correctly and hang correctly, giving you either the sleek or draping look you desire.

One last note: Get several different colors! You'll change your home décor to fit the seasons, so create a tablecloth "wardrobe" to give you plenty of options, including different colors of cloth napkins: white, cream, colored, even monogrammed if you wish.

Table Linens

Registered at: _____

Web site: _____

Formal tablecloth size: _____

Formal tablecloth shape:_____

Casual tablecloth size: _____

Casual tablecloth shape: _____

Item	Brand and Design Name	Color	Quantity Desired	Registered For	Received
Chair pad					
Chair slipcovers					
Napkin rings					
Napkins, casual linen					
Napkins, formal linen					
Placemats					

Item	Brand and Design Name	Color	Quantity Desired	Registered For	Received
Runner, accent tables					
Runner, dining room table					
Table pad					
Tablecloth, casual					
Tablecloth, formal					
Tablecloth for accent tables					
Tablecloth overlay					
Other					

Living Room Linens

Registered at:_____

Web site: _____

Sofa size: _____

Item	Brand and Design Name	Color	Quantity Desired	Registered For	Received
Area rugs					
Hearth rugs					
Pillow shams					
Quilts and blankets					
Slipcovers for ottomans					
Sofa slipcover					
Throw blankets					
Other					

Chapter 24

Window Treatments

Interior decorators say that a change of window treatments can bring a room to life. The right gorgeous new shade can open up a room, making it look bigger. A deeper color can add more sensuality to a space, and a great, touchable fabric brings a high level of luxury to any area.

Add in the hot new looks in wooden slat blinds, decorative bi-level shades, and automatic blinds that sweep open at the touch of a button, and your windows become a form of art in the room.

In this chapter, you'll design your own window treatments, choosing from wispy sheers or lush brocades, eyelet laces, or dramatically draping valances. Most important is choosing the correct sizes for each of your windows, so take a measuring tape to each window in your home, deciding if your design calls for a length to meet the windowsill or stretching down to the floor. Window treatments are sold in width and length varieties, so know your dimensions and take good notes.

Getting Your Numbers Right

How many drapes should you buy? Usually, it's two panels per window for standard-size openings. But you might have a glorious picture or bay window to dress. Three or four panels for these spaces can give the perfect look. Measure well, imagine the sweep of the fabric, the movement of the fabric in the breeze of an open window, the amount of privacy you want for each room (very important), and the amount of sunlight you wish each window treatment to allow in.

A Word About Color

The colors you choose for both your blinds—light wood or dark wood—and your curtains—airy light pastels or deep, rich jewel tones—make all the difference in the look of your room. If you're combining your two households, your choice of window treatments could be all you need to tie in your own separate design styles to a unified whole. Remember this when choosing your own color palette for your windows, and know that it's the wisest move possible to register for *two or three different sets of curtains*.

This gives you the seasonal choice of pastel for spring and summer, and then a coordinating fall and winter look in deeper tones and richer fabrics. You can change the look and feel of each room when you have a second or third set of curtains to hang. There's no such thing as having too many options, so register for multiple sets.

Finally, don't forget to look at your curtain rods. We've come a long way from decades-old white metal curved curtain rods, the house standard. Now, you can choose from thick, carved wooden curtain rods; dual-level rod arrangements with one hanging higher and the other at midlength for shape and architectural accent; ornate metal curtain rods with decorative accents, twists, and elaborate peaks and swirls. They're not kidding when they call it "dressing your windows." You have a tremendous amount of creativity and personal expression open to you here, so look at both home décor stores like Bed Bath & Beyond and home remodeling stores like Home Depot for the latest styles and designs in shades, blinds, and curtains. Custom-cut shades and blinds are usually the order of the day, so always indicate dimensions when you register.

How Do You Register for Custom-Cut Blinds?

You absolutely can register for custom measurement items, and if your guests aren't up to standing at the cutting booth in Home Depot for the perfect width of shades, then this is an ideal use for a gift card you've received. The two of you can go for the cutting session yourselves.

Living Room Window Treatments

Registered at:_____

Web site: _____

Size dimensions:_____

Item	Brand or Design Name	Color	Quantity Desired	Registered For	Received
Blinds					
Curtain panels, first set					
Curtain panels, second set					
Curtain rods					
Finials					
Shades					
Sheers, first set					
Sheers, second set					
Tiebacks (pair)					
Valances, drape or balloon					
Other					
Other					
Other					
Other					
Other					
Other					
Other					
Other					

Dining Room Window Treatments

Registered at:_____

Web site: _____

Size dimensions: _____

Item	Brand or Design Name	Color	Quantity Desired	Registered For	Received
Blinds					
Curtain panels, first set					
Curtain panels, second set					
Curtain rods					
Finials					
Shades					
Sheers, first set					
Sheers, second set					
Tiebacks (pair)					
Valances, drape or balloon					
Other					
Other					
Other					

Bedroom Window Treatments

Registered at:_____

Web site: _____

Size dimensions: _____

Item	Brand or Design Name	Color	Quantity Desired	Registered For	Received
Blinds					
Curtain panels, first set					
Curtain panels, second set					
Curtain rods					
Finials					
Shades					
Sheers, first set					
Sheers, second set					
Tiebacks (pair)					
Valances, drape or balloon					
Other					
Other					
Other					

Guest Room Window Treatments

Registered at:_____

Web site: _____

Size dimensions: _____

Item	Brand or Design Name	Color	Quantity Desired	Registered For	Received
Blinds					
Curtain panels, first set					
Curtain panels, second set					
Curtain rods					
Finials					
Shades					
Sheers, first set					
Sheers, second set					
Tiebacks (pair)					
Valances, drape or balloon					
Other					
Other					
Other					

Bathroom #1 Window Treatments

Registered at:_____

Web site: _____

Size dimensions:_____

Item	Brand or Design Name	Color	Quantity Desired	Registered For	Received
Blinds					
Curtain panels, first set					
Curtain panels, second set					
Curtain rods					
Finials					
Shades					
Sheers, first set					
Sheers, second set					
Tiebacks (pair)					
Valances, drape or balloon					
Other					
Other					
Other					

Bathroom #2 Window Treatments

Registered at:_____

Web site: _____

Size dimensions:_____

Item	Brand or Design Name	Color	Quantity Desired	Registered For	Received
Blinds					
Curtain panels, first set					
Curtain panels, second set					
Curtain rods					
Finials					
Shades					
Sheers, first set					
Sheers, second set					
Tiebacks (pair)					
Valances, drape or balloon					
Other					
Other					
Other					

Kitchen Window Treatments

Registered at:_____

Web site: _____

Size dimensions: _____

Item	Brand or Design Name	Color	Quantity Desired	Registered For	Received
Blinds					
Curtain panels, first set					
Curtain panels, second set					
Curtain rods					
Finials					
Shades					
Sheers, first set					
Sheers, second set					
Tiebacks (pair)					
Valances, drape or balloon					
Other					
Other					
Other					

Home Office Window Treatments

Registered at:_____

Web site: _____

Size dimensions: _____

Item	Brand or Design Name	Color	Quantity Desired	Registered For	Received
Blinds					
Curtain panels, first set					
Curtain panels, second set					
Curtain rods					
Finials					
Shades					
Sheers, first set					
Sheers, second set					
Tiebacks (pair)					
Valances, drape or balloon					
Other					
Other					
Other					

Additional Room Window Treatments

Registered at:_____

Web site: _____

Size dimensions:_____

Item	Brand or Design Name	Color	Quantity Desired	Registered For	Received
Blinds					
Curtain panels, first set					
Curtain panels, second set					
Curtain rods					
Finials					
Shades					
Sheers, first set					
Sheers, second set					
Tiebacks (pair)					
Valances, drape or balloon					
Other					
Other					
Other					

Additional Items for Your Registry

Sign up for a fabric steamer—a handheld device that you'll safely use to "magic wand" away any wrinkles in your curtains, as well as a terrific feather duster that allows you to sweep easily through your slatted blinds for a clean finish.

Chapter 25

Furniture

eed a new sofa? Do you wish to upgrade that twenty-year-old armchair? Need a whole bedroom set or an armoire? Consider the furniture you'll register for, knowing that it makes for a terrific group gift pick.

Again, be sure you have sizes, colors, brand names, and design styles clearly marked on your registry so that you're not at the design whims of your guests.

Furniture

Registered at: _____

Web site: _____

Item	Brand or Design Name	Color	Size	Quantity Desired	Registered For/Received
Area rug					
Arm chair					
Armoire					
Baker's rack					
Bar					
Bed, guest					
Bed, master					
Bedside tables					
Bookcase unit(s)					

Item	Brand or Design Name	Color	Size	Quantity Desired	Registered For/Received
Buffet table					
Chairs, barstools					
Chairs, dining room					
Chairs, kitchen					
Chairs, recliner					
China hutch					
Coffee table					
Desk(s)					
Desk chair(s)					
Dining table and chairs					
Dresser(s)					
End table(s)					
Entertainment center					
Folding chairs					
Folding tables					
Kitchen counter stools					
Kitchen island					
Ottoman(s)					
Recliner					
Rocking chair					
Sofa					
Sofa bed					
Trundle bed					
Workspace tables					
Other					
Other					

Chapter 26

Home Entertaining Items

Consider this chapter the section where you're looking at the fun "toys" for entertaining in your home. And don't be surprised about seeing a Sony PlayStation or Xbox on this list . . . these game systems are gaining in popularity on bridal registries. The couple who plays together, after all, stays together.

"He must have slipped out of sight for two minutes while we were registering in the store. Before I knew it, we had an Xbox on our registry and of course that's the gift the groomsmen gave us. At first, I was embarrassed, but it's been a lot of fun playing with it together on our nights in. We've even placed some romantic bets on our games!" —Carrie, recent bride

Keep in mind that many couples register for *multiple* CD players or DVD players—one for their bedroom, one for their living room, one for their downstairs den, and so on. You're not limited to just one.

The Growing Trend in Electronics

Bridal Guide magazine's recent registry survey shows that in many areas, more couples plan to register for their electronics than buy them. Keep in mind, the numbers are *growing* right now, so what you're looking at is the start of a hot new trend. We already own a lot of our electronics before we get married and can choose to upgrade them now at the time of registry, or upgrade them in the future. These numbers will be much higher in years to come.

Item	Have It Already	Registered for It	We'll Buy It Ourselves
Camera	62.0%	18.0%	10.4%
Computer/laptop	55.6%	10.8%	23.2%
Digital camera	35.6%	34.0%	17.6%
Digital video camera	23.2%	36.4%	20.0%
DVD player	65.2%	15.2%	11.2%
Sound system	47.2%	16.0%	23.2%
Television	68.4%	13.2%	12.0%
VCR	72.4%	8.0%	9.2%
Wireless phone	62.8%	13.2%	12.0%

Home Entertaining Items

Registered at: _____

Web site: _____

Item	Brand Name	Quantity Desired	Registered For	Received
Camcorder				
Camcorder accessory set				
CD player				
Digital camera				
Digital camera accessory set				
DVD player				
Game station accessories (driving wheel, etc.)				
Home computer				

Item	Brand Name	Quantity Desired	Registered For	Received
Movie DVD collections				
Music CD collections				
Portable CD player				
Portable television set				
Sound system				
Speakerphone				
Telephone sets				
Telescope				
Television set				
TiVo subscription				
TiVo system				
VCR				
Xbox or game station				
Xbox or game station games				
Other				
Other				
Other				
Other				
Other				
Other				

Chapter 27

The Bathroom Oasis

The overwhelming trend when it comes to bathrooms is the spa experience. Everyone wants luxury, a calming atmosphere, candles surrounding the bathtub, and heavenly soft towels. It's not just a functional room; it's an oasis of calm. And decorating the bathroom has become every bit as exciting and important as decorating the bedroom.

From color schemes of relaxing sage greens to light yellows, earthy tones of cinnamon or browns and tans, today's bathroom registries are all about creating an environment. In this chapter, you'll create your registry wish list for all the designs and items you'll need for your master bathroom and your secondary bathrooms.

Ultra-Soft Towels

Bath sheets and towels of 100 percent Egyptian cotton are tops on most registry lists, as they provide that indulgent spa feeling. Make an in-store visit to actually feel the softness and texture that will be right next to your skin every day.

How many towels should you register for? It depends on how often you wish to do laundry. Most couples register for six to eight towels—four bath sheets and four washcloths—but it's a terrific idea to register for even more per bathroom. Consider those your minimum figures.

Bridal Guide says . . . 24.4 percent of their surveyed couples already own their own towels, 75.6 percent have signed up for the luxurious new set, and only 3.6 percent of couples plan to buy towels on their own.

Master Bathroom

Registered at: _____

Web site: _____

Item	Brand Name/ Style	Color	Quantity Desired	Registered For	Received
Bath mat					
Bath rug					
Bath towels					
Bathrobes and slippers					
Decorative towels					
Hand towels					
Oversized bath towels					
Shower curtain					
Shower curtain liner					
Shower curtain rings					
Shower curtain rod					
Washcloths					
Other					
Other					
Other					

Guest Bathroom

Registered at: _____

Web site: _____

Item	Brand Name/ Style	Color	Quantity Desired	Registered For	Received
Bath mat					
Bath rug					
Bath towels					
Bathrobes and slippers					
Decorative towels					
Hand towels					
Oversized bath towels					
Shower curtain					
Shower curtain liner					
Shower curtain rings					
Shower curtain rod					
Washcloths					
Other					
Other					
Other					

Bathroom Accessories: Master Bathroom

Registered at: _____

Web site: _____

Item	Brand Name/ Style	Color	Quantity Desired	Registered For	Received
Bath salt set					
Bath scale					
Bathroom drawer organizer set					
Bathtub caddy					
Bathtub jet system					
Clothes hamper					
Cosmetics caddy					
Cosmetics mirror					
Cotton ball holder					
Cotton swab holder					
Curling iron					
Cushioned vanity chair					
Decorative wall hardware					
Electric shaver					
Electric toothbrush					
Fog-proof mirror					
Hair dryer					
Jewelry dish					
Lotion dispenser					

Item	Brand Name/ Style	Color	Quantity Desired	Registered For	Received
Paraffin wax system					
Room heater, portable					
Shaving cream warmer					
Shower caddy					
Shower head, massaging or waterfall					
Shower shampoo dispenser					
Soap dish					
Spa bath mat					
Spa bath pillow					
Tissue holder					
Toilet brush and holder					
Toothbrush holder					
Towel racks					
Towel warmer					
Trash can					
Wall art and décor					
Water cup					
Other					
Other					
Other					
Other					
Other					

Bathroom Accessories: Guest Bathroom

Registered at: _____

Web site: _____

Item	Brand Name/ Style	Color	Quantity Desired	Registered For	Received
Bath salt set					
Bath scale					
Bathroom drawer organizer set					
Bathtub caddy					
Bathtub jet system					
Clothes hamper					
Cosmetics caddy					
Cosmetics mirror					
Cotton ball holder					
Cotton swab holder					
Curling iron					
Cushioned vanity chair					
Decorative wall hardware					
Electric shaver					
Electric toothbrush					
Fog-proof mirror					
Hair dryer					
Jewelry dish					

Item	Brand Name/ Style	Color	Quantity Desired	Registered For	Received
Lotion dispenser					
Paraffin wax system					
Room heater, portable					
Shaving cream warmer					
Shower caddy					
Shower head, massaging or waterfall					
Shower shampoo dispenser					
Soap dish					
Spa bath mat					
Spa bath pillow					
Tissue holder					
Toilet brush and holder					
Toothbrush holder					
Towel racks					
Towel warmer					
Trash can					
Wall art and décor					
Water cup					
Other					
Other					
Other					

Chapter 28

The Bedroom Oasis

A luxurious bed is an invitation to rest, relax, and escape from the pressures and hassles of everyday life. Climbing in between soft sheets melts your tension away. It's your oasis from the world. Let's begin with tips and design ideas for creating a beautiful bed so that you can enjoy the same bliss.

- *First, choose your linen color scheme.* Do you want all white? Pastels in a soft sage green with forest green accents? Deep jewel tones like sapphire or ruby? Is the black-and-white motif perfect for you? Or do you favor chocolate browns and coppers? Some colors may be more comforting and luxurious, while other colors might be a bit "too much." Get your color palette in mind, choosing a complementary range of lights to darks, judging for yourself just how much contrast in color and pattern you prefer.

- *Decide on the level of masculine/feminine.* You may envision a more floral or Victorian bedroom setting, while your groom is looking at a more neutral look, a room he can feel comfortable in. Together, look through some interior decorating magazines or home décor catalogs, or cruise Web sites, to find the perfect look for your bedroom.

- *Finalize your style.* Will you go sleek and modern, or a Zen-inspired spa feel, a five-star hotel look, French country, a cozy bed-and-breakfast style, or vivid red—a real heart-pumping love den?

Bridal Guide on Bed Linens

The recent *Bridal Guide* registry survey you've been checking out throughout this book has found that 83.2 percent of engaged couples have registered for new bedroom linen sets. Of those couples, 18.4 percent are sticking with what they have, and 5.6 percent want to buy their own. The survey found that 12.4 percent of couples are adding new mattresses to their registry lists as well. Very smart.

Bedroom Essentials

Before we get into your bedroom registry worksheets, here's some inspiration and design ideas for what could be the most important room of your house . . .

Sheets

You've heard enough about luxurious sheet sets to know that 100 percent Egyptian cotton sheets are usually considered the gold standard of sheets. They're soft to the touch, the ultimate indulgence.

Learn About Thread Counts

Before you click to add the first Egyptian cotton sheet sets you see to your registry, take a moment to learn the basics of thread count rules at the Bed Bath & Beyond product guides area: www.bedbathandbeyond.com.

Select *several* sheet sets, color-coordinated, and consider different styles to suit the seasons, such as Supima cotton for the summer and comfy flannel for the winter months. Here are just some of the many possibilities in the most touchable sheets out there:

- Combed Egyptian cotton, in a 500–1,000 thread count
- Luxury sateen in a 100 percent pima cotton, for a bit of shine
- Smooth cotton/silk blends
- Satin charmeuse sheets
- Egyptian cotton jersey sheets in 100 percent combed cotton (You've never felt anything softer! Jersey sheets are a top pick among brides- and grooms-to-be.)
- Egyptian cotton sheets with a faux suede cuff

Bedspreads and Comforters

The overlay on your bed creates the largest focal point in your room, so the design, shine, and feel of your chosen comforter or blanket is important. Whether print or solid, matte or shine, this investment is a worthy one. A quality comforter or bedspread will last for years.

- Select more than one for variety and seasonal style.
- Consider reversible comforters, they might be the answer if you love change, with a solid on one side and a pattern on the other. One purchase, two looks.
- Look at some other cover-up possibilities:
  - White goose down comforters in 300–700 thread counts, feather-light or heavier if you like a little bit of weight covering you
  - White duck down comforters, with a silk blend to the thread count for shine and softness
  - Down fillings, which can be filled in pockets to prevent down "bunching" or movements
  - Organic and non-allergenic fillers to comforters if you have allergies
  - 100 percent cotton flannel comforters in a great range of colors like hunter greens and soft lavenders

Duvet Covers

The new trends in duvet covers bring the sense of touch to the fore-front, with 1,000 thread count sateens adding shine, and the following unique and hot bridal registry choices adding some animal instincts to bedroom design:

- Plush velvets
- Faux Persian lamb
- Faux brown zebra stripes adding some zip to a chocolate mocha bedroom
- Faux mink or chinchilla for luxurious softness
- Microsuedes
- Chenille and woven damasks for traditional styles
- Silk dupioni for exceptional shine and smoothness, making a bed look like a present waiting to be unwrapped

Blankets

Add some extra color, a contrasting texture, and a touch of class to your bed design.

- Cashmere in 100 percent cotton is ideal for luxury seekers.
- Cotton thermals and fleeces invite those who want homey warmth and snuggle-ready blankets right out of a bed-and-breakfast environment.
- The warming element of an electric blanket or heated electric mattress cover makes that bed seem to be waiting for you.

Throws

Add another layer of touchable warmth and design with a single or double throw, such as cashmere in a smaller degree, faux fur, faux mink, chenille, a silk blend of 50 percent cotton and 50 percent silk.

Pillows

Before you choose new pillows to replace the same old worn and flat ones you've had for years, visit the Bed Bath & Beyond product guide area (www.bedbathandbeyond.com) for more information on the basics of choosing a great pillow for firmness, thread count, and sizing.

- Consider the best goose down or natural filling pillows.
- Choose specialty pillows that offer extra neck support,

contoured pillows for neck and back health, 100 percent cotton long body pillows to curl around, firm bed wedges and geometric shapes for design—such as circular or oval pillows, and cylindrical pillow rolls.

- Look at textures like velvets, faux furs, sateens, and silks. Today's decorative pillows offer intricate beaded edges, regal tassels, velvet edges, and other touchable, inviting accents.

Shams

Throw some of those extra pillows you've ordered into beautiful shams, mixing up your colors and textures for the ultimate effect. Choose from 100 percent Egyptian cotton, plus all of the fabrics mentioned in the blankets section, for just a little bit more detail.

Dust Ruffles

Dust ruffles may be the most overlooked portion of any bedding ensemble, but these additions provide an all-important finishing touch to your bedding. Without them, your comforter or duvet cover would hang limply over the edge of your bed, not finished to the ground. You'll find matching dust ruffles in sheet sets, or you can finish off your own look with sleek microsuede wraps, eyelet sateens, or fine crochets for a feminine touch.

Canopies

You don't need to own a four-poster bed to have a romantic sheer canopy surrounding your bed. Today's canopy sets come with top loops and attachment gear that you can attach to the ceiling or on a circular bracket above your bed, giving you the *look* of a posted bed without the heavy lifting. With luxurious draping, lots of sheer panels, and golden or corded tassel ties, this is the crowning touch to your beautiful bed.

Bedding Set: Master Bedroom

Registered at: _____

Web site: _____

Item	Brand and Style Name	Color	Quantity Desired	Registered For	Received
Aerobed					
Bed caddy					
Bed lifts					
Blanket, first style					
Blanket, second style					
Canopy set					
Comforter, first style					
Comforter, second style					
Decorative toss pillows					
Dust ruffle, first style					
Dust ruffle, second style					
Duvet clips					
Duvet cover set, first style					
Duvet cover set, second style					
Electric blanket					
Euro shams					
European pillows					
Feather bed					
Fitted sheets, first style					

Item	Brand and Style Name	Color	Quantity Desired	Registered For	Received
Fitted sheets, second style					
Flat sheets, first style					
Flat sheets, second style					
Mattress pad					
Non-allergenic pillow covers					
Pillow protectors					
Pillowcases, first style (sets of 2)					
Pillowcases, second style (sets of 2)					
Pillows					
Room heater, portable					
Sheet clips					
Specialty pillow covers					
Standard shams					
Support and specialty pillows (i.e., neck roll, full body-length pillow)					
Throw, first style					
Throw, second style					
Other					
Other					
Other					

Bedding Set: Guest Bedroom

Registered at: _____

Web site: _____

Item	Brand and Style Name	Color	Quantity Desired	Registered For	Received
Blanket, first style					
Blanket, second style					
Canopy set					
Comforter, first style					
Comforter, second style					
Decorative toss pillows					
Dust ruffle, first style					
Dust ruffle, second style					
Duvet cover set, first style					
Duvet cover set, second style					
Electric blanket					
Euro shams					
European pillows					
Feather bed					
Fitted sheets, first style					
Fitted sheets, second style					
Flat sheets, first style					

Item	Brand and Style Name	Color	Quantity Desired	Registered For	Received
Flat sheets, second style					
Mattress pad					
Non-allergenic pillow covers					
Pillow protectors					
Pillowcases, first style (sets of 2)					
Pillowcases, second style (sets of 2)					
Pillows					
Room heater, portable					
Sheet clips					
Specialty pillow covers					
Standard shams					
Support and specialty pillows (i.e., neck roll, full body-length pillow)					
Throw, first style					
Throw, second style					
Other					
Other					
Other					

Satin Pillowcases

It's true. Beauty experts say that sleeping on satin pillowcases is better for your hair's health and shine. Satin is gentler on your hair, reducing breakage and frizz. It's something to think about when you're planning your bedding registry.

Additional Bedroom Items: Master Bedroom

Registered at: _____

Web site: _____

Item	Brand and Model	Color	Quantity Desired	Registered For	Received
Additional chairs					
Additional tables					
Alarm clock					
Area rugs					
Full-length mirror					
Hope chest/trunk					
Jewelry box					
Tie rack					
Tissue dispenser					
Trash can					
Water pitcher and glass					
Other					
Other					
Other					

Additional Bedroom Items: Guest Bedroom

Registered at: _____

Web site: _____

Item	Brand and Model	Color	Quantity Desired	Registered For	Received
Additional chairs					
Additional tables					
Alarm clock					
Area rugs					
Full-length mirror					
Hope chest/trunk					
Jewelry box					
Tie rack					
Tissue dispenser					
Trash can					
Water pitcher and glass					
Other					
Other					
Other					

Chapter 29

Cleaning and Storage

This might not be the most glamorous category of them all, but you'll certainly appreciate having these handy and helpful items in your home. Countless couples say that registering for a carpet steamer was a smart move and that their closet organizing system made the combining of their two households a snap. What these items lack in flash and luxury they compensate for with their priceless use in the future.

Sign Up for a Spotless Home

Bridal Guide's registry survey says that brides and grooms are signing on for more cleaning items.

Item	We Have It	Registered for It	We'll Buy It Ourselves
Handheld vacuum	31.6%	41.2%	12.4%
Iron	51.6%	32.0%	6.8%
Vacuum cleaner	41.2%	42.8%	8.0%

Notice that the percentages for these items are actually *higher* than for DVD players, VCRs, and cameras!

Cleaning Items

Registered at: _____

Web site: _____

Item	Brand Name or Model	Size	Quantity Desired	Registered For	Received
Air ionizer,					
Air purifier					
Aromatherapy system (i.e., with plug-in scent cartridges)					
Bin liners					
Broom					
Car vacuum					
Carpet steamer					
Cedar hangers					
Cleaning bucket					
Cleaning caddy					
Cleaning gloves					
Cordless power scrubber					
Dust mop					
Dust pan					
Dust rags					
Feather duster					
Garment bags					
Handheld vacuum cleaner					
Humidifier					
Iron					
Ironing board					

Item	Brand Name or Model	Size	Quantity Desired	Registered For	Received
Ironing board cover					
Laundry bags					
Laundry drying rack					
Laundry hampers					
Lingerie laundry bag					
Mesh laundry bags					
Mop system					
Power hose					
Pull-out trash bin					
Recycling buckets					
Silver polishing kit					
Stain removal system					
Step-on trashcan, large					
Step-on trash can, small					
Trash bucket cart on wheels					
Trash buckets					
Upright vacuum cleaner					
Vacuum bags					
Wastebaskets					
Wet vacuum					
Window cleaning squeegee kit					
Other					

Storage and Organizing Systems

Registered at: _____

Web site: _____

Item	Brand Name or Model	Size	Quantity Desired	Registered For	Received
Basement organizer system (for bulk buys, wines or kids' toys)					
Baskets, wire or weave, decorative					
Cap organizer					
Closet organizer system, guest bedroom					
Closet organizer system, home office					
Closet organizer system, living room or den					
Closet organizer system, master bedroom					
Coat hooks					
Crafts organizer system					
Desktop organizing trays					
Drawer organizing trays					
DVD organizer system					
Hanging shoe racks					

Item	Brand Name or Model	Size	Quantity Desired	Registered For	Received
Home safe					
Jewelry organizing system					
Label maker					
Laundry baskets					
Laundry organizer system					
Magazine holders					
Multicolor pens					
Music CD organizer system					
Over-door shoe racks					
Pantry organizer system					
Plastic hangers					
Satin hangers					
Sealed storage bins					
Shoe racks					
Six-tier hangers					
Storage boxes, cardboard and stackable					
Storage boxes, photos and videos					
Sweater racks					
Tie racks					
VHS organizer system					
Wall mount rack					
Wooden shirt hangers					

Item	Brand Name or Model	Size	Quantity Desired	Registered For	Received
Wooden skirt hangers					
Wrapping paper organizer system					
Other					
Other					
Other					

The Basket Craze

You've seen amazing home organizing makeover stories in glossy women's magazines and interior decorating magazines. Photo features show immaculate home offices and dens impeccably organized with specialty baskets lined up on shelving units . . . right next to that hideous "before" picture of the cluttered mess that area used to be. Key to this organizing/décor trend is the storage basket, a beautifully woven pale beige wicker or an intricate Mexican weave in deeper reds. Designers use these baskets to add a homey touch to any room in the house, including bathrooms, and home efficiency experts shout that an organized space leads to peace of mind. Baskets in the perfect sizes could be the home décor and organizing answer for you. So add the following useful types of baskets to your registry list:

- address • bagel • berry • bread • brownie • cake
- cannister • clip keeper with magnetic top • coaster
- corner • craft/knitting • hamper • jewelry and change keeper • key holder • knicknack • magazine • market (basket with handles) • newspaper • pen/pencil • picnic
- recipe file • seedling planter • snack servers • storage with lid • TV remote organizing • tea • tissue • vanity
- weekender

Important for Every Home

Registered at: _____

Web site: _____

Item	Brand Name or Model	Size	Quantity Desired	Registered For	Received
Carbon monoxide detectors					
Escape ladders					
Fire extinguishers					
First aid kit, car					
First aid kit, home					
Flashlights					
Home security system					
Nightlights (important safety item when guests stay in your home!)					
Nonskid tabs for underneath area rugs					
Nonslip tub stickers or strips					
Security sensor lights (outdoors)					
Smoke detectors					
Stand-up ladder					
Step ladder					
Walkie-talkies					
Water filtration systems					
Other					
Other					

Luggage

As you read earlier, a great set of matching luggage is a top choice for wedding registries. Today's new styles and designs—those helpful wheels and handles, specially designed storage pockets, and hidden compartments—all add up to a vast improvement on your old, mismatched set, and now is the time to indulge in a top-notch set for all your future travels and adventures. Research the best sizes and features for you, making sure you each get a smaller weekend suitcase as well as a larger suitcase for longer trips. Look into carryon styles and overnight bags, whatever suits your travel plans now and onward.

Luggage

Registered at: _____

Web site: _____

Item	Brand or Design Name	Color	Quantity Desired	Registered For	Received
Airplane slippers					
Attaché case					
Backpack					
Beach bag					
Carryon bag					
Cushioned neck pillow					
Eye mask					
Fabric shoe bags					
Garment bag					
Hip bag					
Laptop carrying case with accessory pockets					
Luggage rack for the car					

Item	Brand or Design Name	Color	Quantity Desired	Registered For	Received
Luggage strap					
Luggage tags					
Organizer pouch (for cosmetics, etc.)					
Suitcase, large					
Suitcase, medium					
Suitcase, small					
Travel alarm clock					
Other					
Other					
Other					

Chapter 30

Tools and Home Repair

Brides of decades past would fall over at the idea of registering for (gulp) a power drill or circular saw, but today's savvy and home-interested couples are just as thrilled at receiving top-of-the-line tool sets as they are top-of-the-line juicers and toasters. Remember, those home improvement shows are all the rage right now, and you, too, might be talking with one another about redoing the basement, adding an addition, or finally getting that new screen door in place for the back deck.

With tools that you'll keep forever, these particular wedding gifts keep giving and giving. You might sign on at Home Depot or Lowe's, Target or Wal-Mart, or even at a specialty store near you.

Just One Hint

Before you do sign on at a home renovation store, check to make sure your bridal registry is accessible in the store itself. Some companies *don't* have in-store registry counters but rather maintain their registry systems completely online. That is, you sign up for items online, and your guests will shop from your list only online. No in-store printout to shop from. Be sure to check this status first.

Power Tools

Registered at: _____

Web site: _____

Item	Brand or Model Name/Number	Quantity Desired	Registered For	Received
Air compressor				
Biscuit joiner				
Circular saw				
Cordless combination kit				
Cordless drill				
Cordless screwdriver				
Drill				
Drill press				
Generator				
Grinder				
Jigsaw				
Lathe				
Planer				
Power paint roller				
Rotary tool				
Router				
Sander				
Saw				
Soldering set				
Wet/dry vac				
Other				
Other				
Other				

Hand Tools

Registered at: _____

Web site: _____

Item	Brand or Model Name/Number	Quantity Desired	Registered For	Received
Allen wrench set				
Bow saw				
Broom				
Clamp set				
Complete hand tool set				
Complete power tool set				
Cutting knives with extra blades				
Drop cloths				
Extension cords				
Fasteners				
Hammer set				
Hand saw				
Hand truck, convertible				
Hand truck (also called a "dolly"), standup				
Level, laser				
Level, regular				
Marking tool				
Measuring tape				
Paint brushes				
Paint rollers				

Item	Brand or Model Name/Number	Quantity Desired	Registered For	Received
Paint sprayer				
Paint trays				
Painter's tape				
Pliers				
Protective earplugs or headset				
Protective gloves				
Protective goggles				
Saw				
Sawhorses				
Screwdrivers, flat head				
Screwdrivers, Phillips head				
Sets of nails, screws, hooks, etc.				
Socket wrench set				
Surge protector				
Tire pressure gauge				
Toolbox				
Tool storage trunk				
Wrench set				
Other				
Other				
Other				

A Well-Manicured Lawn

Bridal Guide magazine's most recent bridal registry survey turned up some interesting figures. Among them, that 20.8 percent of couples registered for a lawn mower, almost as many as registered for microwaves or honeymoons! So, join the trend and list some must-haves for your outdoor tasks.

Outdoor and Gardening Tools

Registered at: _____

Web site: _____

Item	Brand or Model Name/Number	Quantity Desired	Registered For	Received
Blower				
Bow saw				
Broom				
Bulb planter				
Car wash set				
Chainsaw				
Chipper				
D-handle saw				
Edger				
Extension cords				
Garden caddy				
Garden gloves				
Garden hand tools				
Garden hose				
Garden hose attachments				

Item	Brand or Model Name/Number	Quantity Desired	Registered For	Received
Garden hose rack or hanger				
Garden tractor/ attachments				
Gas can				
Grass shears				
Hedge trimmers				
Hoe				
Lawn mower, push				
Lawn mower, riding				
Lawn watering system				
Lighting system, landscape, walkways, borders, driveway				
Machete				
Pickax/mattock				
Pool cleaning tools				
Pool water testing kit				
Post hole digger				
Pressure washer				
Pruners				
Rakes				
Riding mower				
Round point shovel				
Shovels				
Snowblowers				
Spade				
Spading fork				

Item	Brand or Model Name/Number	Quantity Desired	Registered For	Received
Spray bottles (for weed solutions, etc.)				
Spreader (for grass seed, etc.)				
Square point shovel				
String trimmer				
Tiller/cultivator				
Trenching shovel				
Watering can				
Wheelbarrow				
Other				
Other				
Other				

Chapter 31

Backyards and Patios

As mentioned earlier, backyard patios have become an extension of our living rooms, with more couples looking forward to entertaining guests outdoors in the warm summer and autumn nights. So, the backyard oasis becomes an enormous new category for bridal registries. It's a whole new "room" to design and fill with your choice of wedding gifts.

Imagine terrific barbecue parties out on your deck, cocktails by poolside, informal picnics on your sprawling lawn, a spontaneous flag football game taking place in your yard, everyone hanging out in your pool or hot tub with fresh frozen margaritas served on trays. See chapter 4 for more inspiration on the outdoor entertainment center, and start building your registry wish list right here . . .

Fire Up the Grill!

According to *Bridal Guide* magazine's annual registry survey, 37.2 percent of engaged couples registered for a gas grill or barbecue, whereas 22.4 percent planned to buy this item themselves. Of those surveyed, 33.2 percent already owned their own grill.

Backyard and Patio

Registered at: _____

Web site: _____

Item	Brand or Model Name/Number	Color	Quantity Desired	Registered For	Received
Acrylic pitcher					
Acrylic place settings					
Adirondack chairs					
Ashtrays					
Bar stools					
Barbecue grill					
Barbecue grill cleaning set					
Barbecue grill tool set (basting brush, spatula, tongs, knife, tenderizer, etc.)					
Barbecue grill tool set caddy or storage box					
Beach bag					
Beach chairs					
Beach lounge chairs					
Beach or music CD collection					
Birdbath					
Birdhouse					
Citronella candles					
Cooler					
Décor pillars					
Décor tables					

Item	Brand or Model Name/Number	Color	Quantity Desired	Registered For	Received
Décor urns					
Décor wall hangings					
Earthenware place settings					
Extension cords					
Exterior lighting set					
Fence supplies					
Fryer					
Garden benches					
Garden flags					
Garden materials (tomato plants, herb garden, seedlings, flower seeds)					
Garden stones					
Gazebo					
Glass pitcher					
Hammock					
Hammock pillow					
Hammock stand					
Hummingbird feeder					
Hurricane lamps					
Landscaping materials (rose bushes, flower bulbs, sod, etc.)					
Margarita set					
Mist fans					
Mosquito repellant system					
Outdoor ceiling fan					
Outdoor clock					

Item	Brand or Model Name/Number	Color	Quantity Desired	Registered For	Received
Outdoor fireplace					
Outdoor music system (i.e., waterproof MP3 player)					
Oversized beach towel sets					
Patio table chairs					
Patio table set					
Patio table umbrella					
Picnic basket					
Picnic blanket					
Pillar candles and holders					
Porch swing					
Portable bar					
Portable refrigeration unit					
Recycling bins					
Rotisserie set					
Seafood baskets					
Seafood grilling grid					
Serving platters					
Shade tent					
Shish kebab set					
Smoker					
Solar lighting systems					
Storage building or shed					
Storage caddy or in-shed organizing system					

Item	Brand or Model Name/Number	Color	Quantity Desired	Registered For	Received
String lighting system (for in trees, etc.)					
Thermometer					
Tiki torches					
Trash bin					
Trellis					
Water gardens and pond kits					
Weather-proof chair cushions					
Wind chimes					
Wine tub					
Other					
Other					
Other					
Other					
Other					

Outdoor Party "Toys"

Part of the fun of your outdoor parties—planned or spontaneous—is the games your guests (or just the two of you) will play. Your yard will become *the* place to be, both for classy cocktail parties and laid back volleyball games with hot dogs and beer on the menu. Your friends will gather more often when you provide the ideal setting, as will his friends, and both your families alike. Here are the top "toys" to register for, even more delightful and surprising gift options for your guests to choose from. They'll undoubtedly think, "That's so *them*!" and they'll undoubtedly enjoy using these toys themselves the next time you throw a party.

Outdoor Party "Toys"

Registered at: _____

Web site: _____

Item	Brand or Model Name/Number	Color	Quantity Desired	Registered For	Received
Archery set					
Badminton set					
Basketball set					
Bocce ball set					
Croquet set					
Flag football set					
Frisbee set					
Golf driving net					
Horseshoes set					
Inflated balls (softer versions for volleyball and dodgeball)					
Kids' lawn toys					
Lawn darts set					
Mini golf set, with plastic "holes" and "hazards"					
Pool floats					
Pool games					
Pool volleyball net					
Remote control cars and planes					
Rollerblades					
Softball set					
Supersoakers					
Tetherball set					

Item	Brand or Model Name/Number	Color	Quantity Desired	Registered For	Received
Tree swing					
Volleyball net					
Volleyballs					
Water guns					
Wiffle ball set					
Other					
Other					
Other					

Chapter 32

Sporting Goods and Active Lifestyle Supplies

Sporting goods, like kayaks and mountain bikes, are top picks for today's active and adventurous wedding couples. If you both love to spend the day hiking, boating, biking, or blading, if you regularly play golf together, if you are as far from being "couch potatoes" as they come, then you're going to have lots of fun with this chapter.

Where to Register for Active Gear

Although you can find terrific items at Target and Wal-Mart, biking accessories at Bed Bath & Beyond, and any number of sporting goods through Amazon.com, the one must-see Web site on today's couples' recommendation lists is www.rei.com. After visiting each of the above you should be ready to register your favorites.

Sporting Goods

Registered at: _____

Web site: _____

Item	Brand or Model Name/Number	Color	Quantity Desired	Registered For	Received
Backpacks					
Balance ball					
Bike air pump					
Bike rack					
Binoculars					
Boat rack					
Boat trailer and hitch					
Canoes					
Cyclometer					
Elbow, knee, and wrist pads					
Exercise equipment					
First aid kits					
Global positioning systems					
Golf accessory sets					
Golf bags					
Golf club cleaning kit					
Golf clubs, individual specialty clubs					
Golf clubs, sets					
Golf shoes					

Item	Brand or Model Name/Number	Color	Quantity Desired	Registered For	Received
Hand weights					
Heart rate monitor					
Helmets					
Hiking boots					
Horseback riding accessories					
In-line skates					
Kayaks					
Mountain bikes					
Pedometer					
Polo sets					
Racquet holders					
Racquetball rackets					
Recumbent cycle					
Road bikes					
Running log					
Ski rack					
Skis					
Snowboards					
Snowshoes					
Stationary bicycle					
Sunglasses					
Tennis racquets					
Travel journal					
Treadmill					
Volleyball sets					
Water bottles					
Weight bench and weight set					

Item	Brand or Model Name/Number	Color	Quantity Desired	Registered For	Received
Yoga accessories					
Other					
Other					
Other					

They Can Do That?

One couple set up a financial registry for their active lifestyle—they hired a company to design and build a golf-putting range in their backyard. The "course" had three greens, sand traps, and water hazards all stretching around their in-ground pool. And they used the rest of the money in their account to pay for their exclusive golf club membership and round fees. Talk about a shared passion for the game!

Camping and Traveling Equipment

Registered at: _____

Web site: _____

Item	Brand or Model Name/Number	Color	Quantity Desired	Registered For	Received
Backpacks					
Binoculars, compact					
Binoculars, full size					
Bivy packs					
Camping cookware					
Camping dinnerware					

Item	Brand or Model Name/Number	Color	Quantity Desired	Registered For	Received
Camping flatware					
Camping tent, larger					
Camping tent, two-person					
Camping tour guide books					
Camping tour guide CD-ROMs					
Cleaning/drying racks					
Comfort shoulder straps for duffels and packs					
Compass					
Digital camera					
Duffel bag					
Energy bars, variety packs (one case)					
First aid kit					
Flashlight					
Flasks					
Global positioning system					
Grill accessories					
Grill-top coffeemaker					
Headlamps					
Hiking boots					
Hydration packs					
Inflatable air mattress					

Item	Brand or Model Name/Number	Color	Quantity Desired	Registered For	Received
Inflatable air mattress pump					
Inflatable air mattress sheets					
Insulated mugs and cups					
Lantern accessories					
Lanterns, candle					
Lanterns, fuel					
Locking knives					
Men's outerwear					
Mosquito netting system					
Pack covers					
Personal care item kit					
Personal locator beacons					
Pillows					
Portable grill					
Portable stove and fuel					
Radio					
Replacement bulbs and batteries					
Sealing food containers					
Sleeping bag self-inflating foam pad					
Sleeping bag soft pad					

Item	Brand or Model Name/Number	Color	Quantity Desired	Registered For	Received
Sleeping bags, down					
Sleeping bags, synthetic					
Stuff sack (for laundry, etc.)					
Sunblock (one case)					
Sunglasses					
Swiss army knife					
Tarp shelter					
Tent accessories, stakes and mallet					
Tent ground cover					
Travel journal					
Trekking poles					
Waist packs					
Walkie-talkies					
Water bottles					
Water cooler					
Water purification system					
Waterproof matches					
Waterproof sport watches					
Women's outerwear					
Other					
Other					
Other					

Chapter 33

Home Office Supplies

Your "home office" could be the actual office where you run your own mini-empire, or it could be a desk in a laundry room where you balance your checkbook. Whatever the size, scope, and designer décor of your own personal workspace, you'll need the essentials. And your registry is the perfect opportunity to load up on office equipment, supplies, furniture, and organizing gear.

A growing percentage of the national workforce is self-employed, working from home either full- or part-time. Companies are granting their employees flex time and at-home workdays. So the home office is a swiftly growing point of focus for many people, not just brides- and grooms-to-be. That means there's *great* stuff on the market—stylish office accessories, mahogany desk sets, ergonomic desk chairs, and top-of-the-line office equipment and handheld wireless gadgets. Some couples who have lived together for years do focus their registries *primarily* on their dream home office, in much the same way that brides of previous decades focused on their kitchens and bedrooms.

> *"I've always watched those 'homes of the stars' television shows, and since I am a celebrity wannabe, I also check out the magazines to see how the stars have their home offices decorated. It's amazing. I always wanted my home office to look like Oprah Winfrey's with lots of flowers, great artwork, and books. So I'm using those pictures to plan my own registry list."* —Stacy, bride-to-be

If you plan to spend most of your days (if not some nights and weekends) in your home office, you're registering for a primary room in your home. This environment surrounds you for most of your day.

So, make it functional, comfortable, stylish, and the perfect place to work. After all, even top corporations study the effects of office setup and environment on worker productivity. With calmer décor colors, the right layout, plenty of sunlight, and easy function, your home office could make your own career performance that much better.

Office Furniture

Registered at: _____

Web site: _____

Item	Model and Design Name	Color or Size	Quantity Desired	Registered For	Received
Additional chairs					
Bookshelves					
Coffee tables					
Computer desk					
Couch					
Desks					
Drafting table					
End tables					
Filing cabinets					
Lamps					
Lighting system					
Office chair					
Ottoman					
Printer stand					
Storage bins					
Storage shelving unit					
Tables for office equipment					
Other					
Other					

Office Equipment

Registered at: _____

Web site: _____

Item	Brand Name and Style Number	Color	Quantity Desired	Registered For	Received
Bulletin boards					
Color photocopier					
Computer system					
Cordless phone system					
Desktop accessories					
Digital assistant					
Digital camera					
Dry-erase boards					
Fax machine					
Printer					
Rolodex system					
Scanner					
Shredder					
Speaker phone system					
Speakers					
Web cam					
Zip drive					
Other					
Other					
Other					
Other					
Other					
Other					

Office Supplies

Registered at: _____

Web site: _____

Item	Brand Name and Size	Color	Quantity Desired	Registered For	Received
Business cards					
Business letterhead					
Computer disks					
Computer paper					
Computer software					
Envelopes					
Glossy brochure and photo paper					
Highlighter pens					
Ink cartridges					
Labels					
Mouse pad					
Name plate					
Notepads					
Packing tape					
Paper clips					
Pencils					
Pens					
Postage scale					
Rubber bands					
Shipping envelopes					
Other					
Other					
Other					

Office Décor

Registered at: _____

Web site: _____

Item	Brand Name or Model	Color and Size	Quantity	Registered For	Received
Aquarium and supplies					
Area rugs					
Blinds					
Books					
Bud vases					
Candle holders					
Candles					
Candy dish					
Coasters					
Coffee mug					
Coffee warmer					
Framed artwork or diplomas					
Hat rack					
Keepsakes and sentimental items (like a Lucite-boxed autographed baseball)					
Mirror					
Mouse pad					
Photo albums					
Picture frames					
Pillows					
Shadow boxes for specialty items					

Item	Brand Name or Model	Color and Size	Quantity Desired	Registered For	Received
Specialty accent lighting					
Vases					
Wall paint					
Wallpaper border					
Window treatments					
Other					
Other					
Other					

Part Five

SPECIALTY REGISTRIES

The following registry categories reflect the newest trends in independent stores' own bridal registry programs. Although you will find established honeymoon online registries in this part, know that also you can find unique registries at local stores and boutiques near you, an ideal shopping spot for guests who live in your area. Registering at specialty stores gives you one-of-a-kind options you often won't find at traditional chain store or online registries.

Chapter 34

Wines and Cuisine

C heck locally for specialty wine and gourmet shops that run
their *own* bridal registries. These are not chain stores, and
some do not have Web site registries. They're corner stores
with great reputations and loyal clientele who are joined by a
common interest: a sophisticated love of fine wines, champagnes, and
gourmet foods.

Call it a marketing stroke of genius. Fine wine shops and gourmet stores have watched the bridal registry industry grow to the tune
of a 30 percent increase each year. These retailers have their ears to
the ground, keeping track of wedding trends and knowing that fine
wines and great menus are important to brides and grooms. And
they know also that today's wedding couples have great taste.
Modern-day couples love their wines. They travel the world, enjoying amazing cultural cuisines and rituals. They travel to vineyards and
wine country for their vacations. Some even plan their weddings at
a vineyard. What's clear to these store and shop owners is that today's
older and more sophisticated wedding couples, including those plan-

---

Fine Wines on the Scene

Bridal Guide's registry survey says that 10.4 percent of their
responding brides and grooms have added wines to their lists.
The 38.8 percent who say they're going to buy their own are
missing out on a great opportunity here!

---

ning second weddings and thus looking for something more unique in the wedding registry realm, welcome the idea of registering for their own wine cellars and fine collection of vintages.

If you're growing more excited about this idea by the minute, thinking, Yes! A wine cellar! That's perfect for us! you, too, are among the growing percentage of brides and grooms who have expanded their idea of a "bridal registry" to include New Zealand and Chilean reds, Sonoma chards, and the best-rated cabernet sauvignons on the market today.

If you're not already a wine connoisseur, you can become one by spending some time on www.winespectator.com, researching the ins and outs of the wine industry. On this site, you'll learn about the best new vineyards, the best blends, wine and food pairings, the latest award-winning vintages and wine regions to visit . . . perhaps on your honeymoon. Purchase wine books and journals, wine course software, or attend wine education classes at your local fine wine shop.

Couples love learning about wines and champagnes together, especially with an upcoming wedding. They sign up for wine tastings at local vineyards and as part of their vacations. This could be a new world for you to explore together.

A terrific wine shop, with its knowledgeable wine expert, can be your source of choice for their independent registry service. You sign up at the store, led by that wine expert pointing out all the best choices in wines, champagnes, cordials, and liquors, then record your choices. Guests who live nearby—who might have planned to buy you a bottle of great champagne as a wedding gift anyway—will appreciate having your established wish list to shop from.

Check locally to see if there's a wine shop with a registry near you, and if they don't have one . . . suggest that they create one.

Gourmet Food Registries

Also growing in the industry are gourmet food registries, attracting brides and grooms with the promise of personal chef service for a year, monthly dinners delivered to their door, and healthy meals and snacks made by an expert. Included in this are the "food of the month" programs that many gourmet shops run, such as fruit of the month, cheese

Fresh from the Farm

Here's another growing trend . . . signing up for a monthly shipment from a local family farm. These new crop co-ops arrange for you to get a delivery of fresh corn, tomatoes, peppers, eggplant, apples, and other organic homegrown foods, including seasonals like pumpkins and gourds. A year's subscription to this service as part of a farm's new registry service is a terrific way to get your health-conscious, organic menu items delivered right to you. Check out local farms near you to see if they run a registry. If not, consider signing on anyway with some of your wedding gift money.

of the month, steaks of the month, seafood of the month. Your registry could set you up for a monthly shipment of delicious cuisine.

At an independent gourmet store's registry, you can find kitchen essentials for the worldly and sophisticated chef. That means you can sign up for exotic spices, international sauces (like Dutch fondue dipping sauces), sea salts, seafood marinating sauces, ginger teriyaki sauces, imported vegetables and unique fruits, chai teas, flavored coffee syrups, even edible flowers. Your choices for the well-stocked kitchen are endless, including specialty cooking tools, pearlized chop sticks, and chocolate sauces you can use . . . outside the kitchen.

Cooking together might be a shared passion of yours. So look at food and drink as a possible second or third bridal registry option.

Chapter 35

Books and Music and Art

Think about that little art shop in the center of town, the one with the cobalt blue blown glass vases, woven tapestries, handmade candles, crystal eggs, and local artists' paintings in great gilt frames. Perhaps the shop includes beaded curtain accents, handmade cashmere quilts, and mini table lamps with burgundy colored beaded lampshades.

This could be the site of one of your bridal registries, if the shop runs its own gift registry program—which more and more independently owned stores are doing these days. The owners and proprietors of these shops, sometimes artists themselves, know that the big store chain registries offer terrific appliances and mass-produced décor that's fine by some people's standards. But they also know that couples who value artisan work, couples who themselves are unique and expressive, look for unique items. And they want to register for them.

Major magazines featuring celebrities' breathtaking home décor are forever featuring the latest hot starlet's penchant for unique artwork, the ceramic vase from South Africa, the eye-catching painting above the fireplace. These celebrities attend auctions to bid on budding artists' masterpieces, and they're paying a *lot* of money to have an original in their home. They're even buying their artist friends' pieces, turning *them* into household names.

Here is where you, too, can play celebrity stylist, filling your registry with peerless choices. For example, those decorative accents can be the focal point of your room—a low wooden Oriental coffee table or an oversized cutting vase on a foyer table, the ideal curve of a lamp on a reading table, the lineup of Russian dolls on a bookshelf, or the geode half circles set on your fireplace mantel.

Check around for art and unique gift shops that offer their own registry, and sign up for the kinds of décor you'd love to see in your home.

Museum-Quality Art

Couples with a flair for paintings, sculpture, statues, and other fine creations rush to The Metropolitan Museum of Art Store.

Its items for sale and registry are inspired by the museum's collections and could be the perfect source for your home décor. Visit www.metmuseum.org/store to find the stores and their registries near you.

Books and Music

The first registry that comes to mind when you think about listing books and music is Amazon.com, which could be one of your own primary registry sources for far more than these two categories. Most couples looking at books and music do go the Amazon route, or to www.felicite.com, which also has a great following right now. But also you can find great book and music registries at independent bookstores and music shops. Check around for unique independent bookstores, those utopias for book lovers who adore the overstuffed couches and community programs, the more intimate environments and the friendly personalized knowledge of the fifth-generation bookstore proprietors.

Wherever you find your ideal book and music registry—whether online or around the corner from your office—think about signing on in the following categories.

Books and Music

Registered at: _____

Web site: _____

Item	Title or Artist	Quantity	Registered For	Received
Anthologies, literature				
Anthologies, poetry				
Book series				
Bookmarks				
Books autographed by the author				
Books to support a shared interest or hobby				
Books to support your career				
Car CD storage systems				
CD or DVD cleaners				
CDs, complete collection by one artist				
CDs, new artist release				
CDs, special anniversary edition				
Classical collections				
Coffee table books				
Complete library of novels by one favorite author				
Cultural music				

Item	Title or Artist	Quantity	Registered For	Received
DVDs, special anniversary edition				
Favorite movies				
Jazz collections				
Journals				
Leather-bound set of classic literature				
Mini book light				
Movie soundtracks				
New artist works				
Wine tasting soundtracks				
Other				
Other				
Other				

If you are registering for books and a book series, check out some titles that focus on *marriage*. You'll find a treasure trove of titles that get you asking each other questions about your values and plans for the future, fun questions about your likes and dislikes, even books about adding romance to your every day. You'll also find faith-based titles like *Pure Gold* by Susanne Alexander and Craig Farnsworth that explore the top character qualities essential for a happy and lasting marriage. Now that's a wise investment in your future.

Movies

Included in this category of course is building a movie library. Perhaps you'd like to stock your new DVD collection with a great movie series, documentaries, or the complete seasons of your favorite television shows. Your place is the perfect entertaining site when you have classic movies to pop into your DVD player, or you could find yourselves cuddled together under a blanket for your own movie night in. Once again,

---

Don't Forget . . .

Other boxed DVD sets or series you both want: fitness or yoga DVD or VHS selections, your favorite comedian's television specials, travelogues, and more.

---

turn to Amazon.com or your favorite independent movie source for the top titles you both love, and create your movie library shopping list here.

Wish List: Our Most Wanted Music, Movies, and Books

1. _____	14. _____
2. _____	15. _____
3. _____	16. _____
4. _____	17. _____
5. _____	18. _____
6. _____	19. _____
7. _____	20. _____
8. _____	21. _____
9. _____	22. _____
10. _____	23. _____
11. _____	24. _____
12. _____	25. _____
13. _____	26. _____

Chapter 36

Honeymoon Registries

Imagine registering for a champagne sunset cruise . . . or his and hers massages on the beach . . . scuba diving and swimming with dolphins . . .

That's the allure of the new honeymoon registries that so many couples are enjoying right now. You create a full registry where your guests can buy you a romantic and adventurous experience on your honeymoon, something you'll never forget. Memories last longer than bathroom towels, so the gift truly is priceless. Guests *love* being able to give you something you'll treasure, especially those guests who are romantics at heart and all too eager to help you create the honeymoon of a lifetime.

Bridal Guide's survey says that 24.8 percent of engaged couples in their study have signed on to honeymoon registries, so that's a lot of couples helping themselves to get the vacation of their dreams, packed with adventure and romance.

The Next Best Thing

The honeymoon registry is the ideal second registry you'll set up—in addition to a traditional home supply registry where you can get those towels, sheets, bakeware, and kitchen appliances.

How It Works

As you'll see once you start checking out the many different kinds of honeymoon registries out there (resort, cruise, adventure, etc.), some registry choices are midpriced and as such make for a terrific gift for one guest to buy: like Jet Ski rentals, a horseback ride on the beach at sunset, those his and hers massages. Others are big-ticket items, like your airfare or your weeklong stay at the resort. These more extravagant elements are broken down into "units," such as 10 units of $100 for your five-star hotel suite. Each guest buys 1 unit, like buying a "share" of the gift. On the registry, the status would then be marked as "1 unit fulfilled, still needs 9."

Your stay at the resort, then, could become the perfect group gift, with each participant obtaining for you a share of your accommodations, and the group as a whole enjoying the thrilling satisfaction of making your honeymoon dream come true.

> *"My friends from work all chipped in to buy out the expense of our hotel suite. We were able to get an oceanfront suite with windows that looked out over the horizon, with rainbows over the ocean every morning, an incredible breeze, a canopy bed, and even our own swimming pool out on our terrace. It was just the most incredible place to call 'home' during our honeymoon. We would never have been able to afford that suite—or that experience—on our own."*
> —*Sasha and Sam*

- When you check out any honeymoon registry site, you'll be treated to a list of destinations around the world, complete with expert-designed honeymoon packages.
- Each registry item may be described in detail, giving your guest an exciting look at just what he or she is about to give you. For instance, your suite might be described, or the kayak trip you want could be illustrated as "a daylong kayak trip through the valley, surrounded by colorful red rock canyon walls, and a gourmet lunch stop at the base of a waterfall." Who wouldn't want to give you *that* experience? It's so much more colorful than the simple description of "kayak trip."

- You'll often find an 800 number where you'll reach a honey-moon concierge who will help you tailor your dream vacation right down to where you want to register for special dinners out, spa treatments, tennis lessons, and bottles of champagne sent to your room. It's the star treatment, having your own expert consultant suggesting the best and most popular attractions at the destination and resort you have in mind.

- Some honeymoon registry sites also will help you make your travel arrangements, right down to a car rental or a limousine ride from the airport to your hotel.

- You can register either online or over the phone, making your choices as you wish, and even logging back in (or calling back) to "tweak" your honeymoon registry with additions or changes. It works just like a traditional gift registry, only you're signing up for *experiences*.

- Some registries allow you to create your own personalized home page, complete with photos of you, along with a description and links to your honeymoon registry list.

- For a special touch, some sites encourage you to add personalized notes to the items you've chosen, such as "Jeff loves scuba diving, and we're looking forward to going together for the first time!"

- And at some, you can password-protect your honeymoon registry, keeping your personal listing accessible only to your guests who have the code.

- You can ask to be notified by e-mail when a guest has purchased something from your honeymoon registry, and the choice is yours if you want that e-mail to give you full details of who bought what. If you love surprises, the e-mail notification system can cloak the giver's ID, letting you know only that your airfare is now completely purchased, or that you're getting that tour of the island perfume factory.

- Many registries provide a stack of personalized postcards for you to send out to friends and family, letting them know that you have a honeymoon registry all set up and waiting for them to review.

- Or, you can arrange to send your guests an e-mail announcement with links to your honeymoon registry.
- Guests have the option of purchasing on the online registry or placing their orders by phone or fax.
- Some registries provide the options of financial investment only. That means you have an account not run by individual purchases (like "champagne dinner cruise"), but by dollar credits put toward your registry choices. That is, your guests are kicking in dollar value as if into a savings account or gift card for you to use on your honeymoon. Some of these registries remain active for eighteen months and are renewable as general travel registries. That means that you can store up any "credits" or extra purchases made by guests for future vacations, even your first-anniversary getaway.

All This for Free?

Not always. Some registries may charge a basic setup fee for creating your honeymoon registry, and others have additional charges for helping with "extras" such as your travel plans. You will find that some sites charge a 9 to 15 percent service fee for the total cost of your honeymoon, which is often absorbed into each guest's individual purchases. Included in service fees are the company's phone calls and faxes on your behalf, your concierge's time in helping you research, and other personalized services. Check out stated and hidden fees carefully, including any extra fees posted by the resort or by the individual activities you have requested (such as deposits for those Jet Skis, etc.). You can often arrange your billing schedule for any fees that you incur according to dates *you* set, such as a week before the wedding.

The Sites

This section provides the details on several of the major honeymoon registries available today. By no means are these the *only* choices in existence, so I encourage you to look further on your own. New honeymoon registries are popping up daily, run by resort chains, cruise lines, adventure outing companies, and even bridal Web sites. The trend is growing so quickly now that you'll undoubtedly find a treasure trove of new programs and opportunities set up to help you get the honeymoon of your dreams. Call or log on to the following (remember to add www):

Honeyluna.com (800-809-LUNA[5862]): Perhaps you've heard or read about this site already—it is one of the founders of the trend. With terrific icons for each registry item, descriptions of tours and activities, and the ability to add personalized notes, this site provides the details your guests will love to see for themselves.

Cruise Direct Online: cruisedirect.com (800-365-1445): This top cruise site's bridal registry program activates once you have booked and made a deposit on your honeymoon cruise. At that point, you're all set to create your registry. You'll get a personalized Web site with pictures of you, printed cards with all your registry details, and access to essential information about your cruise vacation. You'll see details on many different cruise lines' sailing schedules and ports of call, activities to choose from, indulgences while on board, honey-mooner specials, even links to individual cruise lines' Web sites so that you can check out the ships, the cabins, the restaurants, the night clubs. If you've never been on a cruise before, helpful articles at this site will give you all the basics.

TheHoneymoon.com (888-796-7772): You'll check out their registry library, plus real couples' sample registries for inspiration, work with a honeymoon specialist, and check out the hottest honeymoon destination rankings. This site also allows you to print out your own honeymoon registry postcards and invitation inserts, plus an e-mail

letter to direct guests to your own complete wedding web page at
this site. You do have an option to create your home page exactly as
you wish, including putting links to your other bridal registries.

TheBigDay.com (800-304-1141):   This site's tools allow you to
customize your registry with your own photos and captions to further detail the items on your list. Along with the same features
described in the previous sites—those postcards and inserts to order,
professional help planning your site, additional travel plans, and the
same secure online purchasing lock—you also get to link your own
personal wedding Web site to this registry.

WeddingChannel.com: You'll find a special bridal registry that
you can activate once you've booked your Sandals or Beaches resort
honeymoon, and you'll then log on to your own free Wedding
Channel.com account for its use, with all the perks described in this
section.

Another angle of the WeddingChannel.com registry is their affil-
iated Starwood Honeymoon registry, with access to over 100 participating hotels and resorts in the following chains: Westin, Sheraton,
Four Points Sheraton, St. Regis, Luxury Collection, and W Hotels.
You'll work with their concierge at 800-503-7800 to locate the ideal
destination, resort, and package within their Honeymoon Collection.
You'll find exciting special packages, such as their Hawaiian Ocean
Romance package (available at the time of this writing) in the tropical islands, at luxurious hotel choices, dining "credits," a fourth or
fifth night *free*, and access to all other member resorts in the area. As
they say, you can "stay at one and play at another." Their Pacific
French Polynesia package gives you seven nights at your hotel, plus
breakfast buffets, spa treatments, a formal gourmet dinner included,
and more. Check the site right now to see which dream vacation
packages they currently offer.

It's an escape just to *read* about these luxury trips, and you'll
surely have plenty to choose from once you start designing your own
personalized honeymoon registry here.

Chapter 37

Charitable Registries

You might be like so many other couples who like to turn their bridal registries into something that "gives a little back." By that, I mean signing on to charitable registries where your guests can make a donation to your favorite charities instead of buying you a traditional wrapped gift for your kitchen, bedroom, or living room. It's what you asked for, after all.

The trend in charitable giving for wedding gifts is on the rise, with more and more couples choosing this option as their second or third registries in addition to their traditional home décor store programs.

> *"We decided to go with a charitable registry, since we both do so much volunteer work and in fact actually met one another during a 5K for The Susan G. Komen Breast Cancer Foundation. It's a part of who we are as a couple, something we value. So, of course we think this is a great option to give to our guests, many of whom have already made nice donations in our names to our favorite causes. We love knowing that we're a part of a good thing." —Nancy and Warren*

Like a traditional registry, you sign up online, select your favorite charities for your guests' donations, and then the site takes care of the rest. You may even be notified by e-mail each time someone makes a donation in your name through your registry, giving you that great feeling of satisfaction every time you check your e-mail. You're doing something great for the world. And so are your guests . . . all because of your decision to set up a charitable registry.

What Will People Think?

Will your guests scoff at the idea of charitable registries? Maybe. Maybe not. Some wedding guests like the idea, but they'd really rather give you something you can use in your home, something that will be useful to you. Reports are that while many couples' charitable registries are accepted enthusiastically, some guests are just warming up to this idea. They haven't fully made peace with the concept of making an online donation and then showing up empty-handed at your wedding. That's why this is a terrific idea for an additional registry option. You'll give guests the choice.

JustGive.org

This giving site's database features over 1 *million* charities to choose from, with a terrific educational and insightful collection of data for each in their "Just Give Guide." For instance, I checked out their category "Animal" and found out that 10 billion animals around the world are killed each year for food and 15 million out of 20 million abandoned animals are euthanized each year. Yikes. That certainly got my attention. I then went on to read about all the *good* that these animal charities accomplish, such as animal adoption programs, funding "no kill" shelters, low-cost spaying and neutering of pets, the establishment and maintenance of animal sanctuaries. I learned about the Animal Welfare Act and the Endangered Species Act, which has successfully brought the American bald eagle, the California condor, and the gray wolf back from the edge of extinction. By looking at a couple's registry, I learned an incredible amount about the need for donations to animal welfare charities, and, yes, I made a donation.

Your guests, then, get an education in something you strongly believe in, they get inspiring news that they *are* helping to make a difference, and they get to be a part of the solution. It's a far different experience and a more lasting feeling of satisfaction than shopping for towels in a department store.

JustGive.org says that the top categories that their wedding couples are choosing to sign up for are:

- **Animals.** Charities such as Best Friends Animal Sanctuary, Fund for Animals, World Wildlife Fund, Humane Society of the U.S., and local animals and rescue groups across the country
- **International relief.** Charities such as Global Fund for Women as well as Doctors Without Borders

Other hot categories include environmental groups and children's charities, homelessness, medical groups searching for cures, education, and arts and culture. The site says it's thrilled to be a conduit to nonprofits that might not otherwise receive money, and it is also a way to encourage all of your guests to support your most cherished *local* charities. That's right—this site includes among its million options many local groups that need help. And with the average donation through JustGive.org at an impressive $70, that's a lot of giving back going on.

Dave and Randi's JustGive.org Registry

David Novakoff and Randi Gerber are a real couple who registered for their wedding on JustGive.org. Their registry opened with a personal message: "Hi everyone . . . we are choosing a charity wedding registry because that would be more meaningful to us than any gift. Also, we don't have room for any more 'stuff' in our little apartment! But seriously, we hope that you will donate to one of our charities . . . we chose them because we feel they are truly doing the right thing and need our support."

The couple also included mention of their personal wedding Web site and their own e-mail addresses in case their guests wished to contact them directly. Their registry then listed the names and descriptions of their chosen charities, along with some personal notes from the two of them ("Alternatively, you could get us a subscription to their magazine!" "If you're not sure which one to pick, pick this one!" and "One of the best animal sanctuaries in existence!"). Here are just some of their favorite charities as listed on their registry:

- Earthwatch Expeditions
- Farm Sanctuary
- Greenpeace International
- Rainforest Action Network
- Wildlife Conservation Society
- World Wildlife Fund, Inc.

Their registry works just like any other registry, with a box to click on and a donation to be typed in.

IDoFoundation.org

This giving site is a little bit different. They have the same official charitable donations feature, which works in the same manner as described earlier with plenty of well-researched and legitimate charities to choose from. And they also have a unique partnership plan, in which your more traditional registries are linked to partner with this site. That means, for instance, for every home décor or kitchen item your guests buy for you through your Linens-n-Things registry (signed on as an affiliate of this site) a percentage of *that* purchase goes to charity. It's like a rewards system, giving a little kickback as an added feature to each purchase.

At the time of this writing, the IDoFoundation.org stated that a certain percentage of each guest's purchase would be donated to your favorite charity at no additional charge to you or your guests. Here are some of their partners:

- Amazon.com
- Cooking.com
- JCPenney
- Linens-n-Things

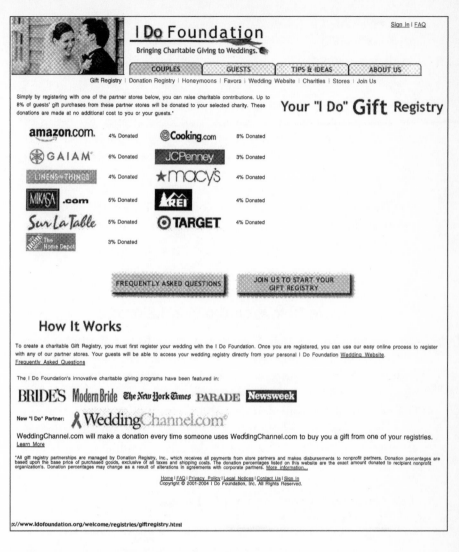

Making your charitable gift registry choices:
www.idofoundation.org/welcome/registries/giftregistry.html

- Mikasa.com
- Rei.com
- Ross-Simons
- Target

Check the list now to see which partnership options are on their site, at which percentages of giving. You could arrange *two* forms of charitable giving within your own registry—traditional cash donations and a donation through the purchase of a traditional wrapped gift.

Like other charitable registries, this site will provide you with your own wedding Web site, where you can link all your registry lists and provide your guests with explanations as to their options and how this site works.

More Details on IDoFoundation.org

Couples who register their weddings with the I Do Foundation have the option of supporting one of their recommended partners or suggesting their own charity of choice. In this way, they provide assistance to couples looking for good groups to support, while giving flexibility to those who already have an organization in mind.

The I Do Foundation says, "The majority of our couples choose to support organizations in the area of children, youth, and families. They are supporting organizations like:

The National Center for Family Literacy
325 West Main Street, Suite 200
Louisville, KY 40202
www.familylit.org
502-584-1133

Mission Statement: NCFL's mission is to expand the number and improve the quality of family literacy services across the nation, creating educational and economic opportunities for parents and children. NCFL's vision maintains that all families at the lowest ends of the literacy and economic continua have opportunities to improve their education, economic status, and social well being through quality family literacy services.

Girls Inc.
120 Wall Street
New York, NY 10005-3902
www.girls-inc.org
212-509-2000

Mission Statement: Inspiring all girls to be strong, smart, and bold.

Children International
2000 E. Red Bridge Road
Kansas City, MO 64131
www.children.org
816-942-2000

Mission Statement: Children International's mission is to help children who live in dire poverty. This is accomplished through the generosity of our contributors by providing children with program benefits and services that meet basic needs, enhance their self-esteem, and raise their physical and educational levels in a meaningful, lasting way.

Beyond these child-centered organizations, our couples have made the organization Doctors Without Borders one of their favorites as well.

Doctors Without Borders
333 7th Avenue, 2nd Floor
New York, NY 10001-5004
www.doctorswithoutborders.org
212-679-6800

Mission Statement: Doctors Without Borders is an independent, private, international medical relief organization that aids victims of armed conflict, epidemics, natural and man-made disasters, and social marginalization. It provides this aid regardless of race, religion, creed, or political affiliation.

Real I Do Foundation Couples Say . . .

"It's a no-brainer. These stores are willing to cooperate, so why not take advantage of it? There's no reason not to! We toyed with just asking for donations, but both of us have lived with roommates for a long time, so we realized there is a lot of stuff we still need. And all of our needs are taken care of with Cooking.com, Linen's-n-Things, Target." —Laura

"Everybody thinks it's a great idea, and some of my friends who had gotten married in recent years wish they could have taken advantage of it. We feel so fortunate to have found each other and to be having this wonderful wedding that we want to share our good fortune with others." —Laura

"This option was fantastic because it's a great opportunity to say we're not totally 'us' centered. We were lucky enough to find each other. You spend so much money for that one day, so it's a good way to be mindful when your day is over to help other people beyond that one day." —Ayanna

"We are deeply involved with the nonprofit world; we both work at nonprofits currently. We share a common passion for social justice and the Asian American community. We thought that the idea of a charitable wedding matched our own life interests and goals very well." —Deepa

"We're having a traditional Indian wedding. That means that the guest list is large, the food will be great, our families are very involved, and the planning is . . . intense! But we also want our union to have resonance beyond our own lives and our families and friends. By hosting a charitable wedding, we know that our coming together has a much bigger impact." —Deepa

"Both of us felt from the beginning that we had all this attention on us, and it was very nice, but we wanted to deflect it a little bit. We didn't need a whole bunch of stuff, but people would want to get us

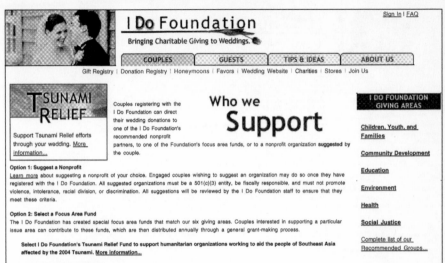

I Do Foundation

Bringing Charitable Giving to Weddings.

COUPLES   GUESTS   TIPS & IDEAS   ABOUT US

Gift Registry I Donation Registry I Honeymoons I Favors I Wedding Website I Charities I Stores I Join Us

TSUNAMI RELIEF

Support Tsunami Relief efforts through your wedding. More information...

Couples registering with the I Do Foundation can direct their wedding donations to one of the I Do Foundation's recommended nonprofit partners, to one of the Foundation's focus area funds, or to a nonprofit organization suggested by the couple.

Who we Support

I DO FOUNDATION GIVING AREAS

Children, Youth, and Families

Community Development

Education

Environment

Health

Social Justice

Complete list of our Recommended Groups...

Option 1: Suggest a Nonprofit
Learn more about suggesting a nonprofit of your choice. Engaged couples wishing to suggest an organization may do so once they have registered with the I Do Foundation. All suggested organizations must be a 501(c)(3) entity, be fiscally responsible, and must not promote violence, intolerance, racial division, or discrimination. All suggestions will be reviewed by the I Do Foundation staff to ensure that they meet these criteria.

Option 2: Select a Focus Area Fund
The I Do Foundation has created special focus area funds that match our six giving areas. Couples interested in supporting a particular issue area can contribute to these funds, which are then distributed annually through a general grant-making process.

Select I Do Foundation's Tsunami Relief Fund to support humanitarian organizations working to aid the people of Southeast Asia affected by the 2004 Tsunami. More information...

Option 3: Select a Recommended Partner
In keeping with the Foundation's mission, and as a service for couples, the I Do Foundation has developed a list of recommended nonprofit partners. All of these organizations reflect the Foundation's goal of supporting progressive organizations working to promote social change in underserved communities. The I Do Foundation's recommended partners are bringing new resources to organizations that are making a difference, especially for low-income people. For more information on our criteria.

Interested in raising wedding donations for your nonprofit? The I Do Foundation is interested in helping a variety of organizations learn how to spread the word about this opportunity. Let us know by using our web form if you'd like to learn more about how your volunteers or supporters can raise donations for your charity.

Spread the Word

Nonprofits: Use the following text to tell your volunteers, donors, and constituents how they can raise funds for your organization through their weddings.

Getting married? Now you can support [organization's name] by registering with the I Do Foundation. From honeymoons to invitations to wedding gifts to charitable wedding favors, the I Do Foundation allows couples and their guests to make wedding-related purchases that generate donations for charity. The I Do Foundation's Donation Registry service also makes it easy for guests to make donations in lieu of gifts. All of these services are available free of cost at www.IDoFoundation.org. Check it out today, and be sure to select [organization's name] as the beneficiary of your charitable wedding.

The I Do Foundation's innovative charitable giving programs have been featured in:

BRIDE'S   Modern Bride   The New York Times   PARADE   Newsweek

New "I Do" Partner: **WeddingChannel.com**

WeddingChannel.com will make a donation every time someone uses WeddingChannel.com to buy you a gift from one of your registries.
Learn More

Charities: www.idofoundation.org/nonprofits/

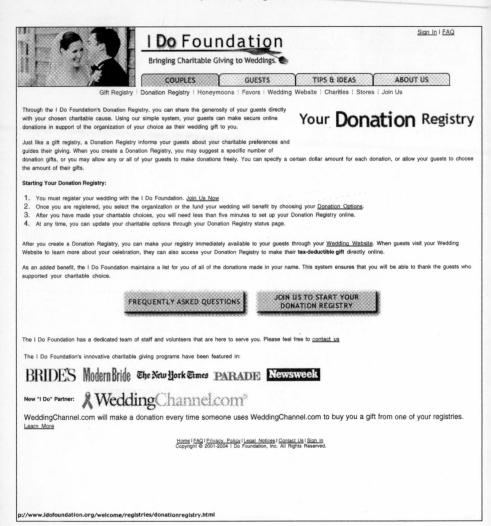

I Do Foundation

Bringing Charitable Giving to Weddings.

COUPLES | GUESTS | TIPS & IDEAS | ABOUT US

Gift Registry | Donation Registry | Honeymoons | Favors | Wedding Website | Charities | Stores | Join Us

Your **Donation** Registry

Through the I Do Foundation's Donation Registry, you can share the generosity of your guests directly with your chosen charitable cause. Using our simple system, your guests can make secure online donations in support of the organization of your choice as their wedding gift to you.

Just like a gift registry, a Donation Registry informs your guests about your charitable preferences and guides their giving. When you create a Donation Registry, you may suggest a specific number of donation gifts, or you may allow any or all of your guests to make donations freely. You can specify a certain dollar amount for each donation, or allow your guests to choose the amount of their gifts.

Starting Your Donation Registry:

1. You must register your wedding with the I Do Foundation. Join Us Now
2. Once you are registered, you select the organization or the fund your wedding will benefit by choosing your Donation Options.
3. After you have made your charitable choices, you will need less than five minutes to set up your Donation Registry online.
4. At any time, you can update your charitable options through your Donation Registry status page.

After you create a Donation Registry, you can make your registry immediately available to your guests through your Wedding Website. When guests visit your Wedding Website to learn more about your celebration, they can also access your Donation Registry to make their **tax-deductible gift** directly online.

As an added benefit, the I Do Foundation maintains a list for you of all of the donations made in your name. This system ensures that you will be able to thank the guests who supported your charitable choice.

FREQUENTLY ASKED QUESTIONS | JOIN US TO START YOUR DONATION REGISTRY

The I Do Foundation has a dedicated team of staff and volunteers that are here to serve you. Please feel free to contact us

The I Do Foundation's innovative charitable giving programs have been featured in:

BRIDE'S   Modern Bride   The New York Times   PARADE   Newsweek

New "I Do" Partner: WeddingChannel.com

WeddingChannel.com will make a donation every time someone uses WeddingChannel.com to buy you a gift from one of your registries.
Learn More

p://www.idofoundation.org/welcome/registries/donationregistry.html

Donation registry:
www.idofoundation.org/welcome/registries/donationregistry.html

gifts, so this was a way to deflect some of the attention to people who could really use it." —Ariane

"I liked the fact that we were able to register for gifts and also pick an organization that had a lot of importance for us. Supporting a local organization that we have a personal connection to is very meaningful for us. I recommend to other couples that this is a great way to have your friends and family support something meaningful for you." —Wendy

"We felt guilty asking people to buy gifts for us. My husband is my biggest present anyway, so I don't need expensive gifts. Plus I have a lot of friends who are getting married, and everyone has this feeling that the old expensive wedding traditions just aren't worth it anymore. You feel selfish spending so much on yourself. Everyone wants to do something to extend wedding money to a cause that's worth it." —Laura

Which Kinds of Charities Do You Support?

You might find, like so many other couples who cruise through these charitable donation sites, that you discover new charities and causes you wish to support. That's a happy side effect of exploring this option—you both may find a new favorite charity to support and volunteer for in the future. A shared goal and values system is a key element to a happy and lasting marriage, so be sure to check out these sites' extensive charity categories and individual listings together. As a team, you can read all about the work each group is doing to reach their goal, check out their recent successes, and even read testimonials from people they've helped.

Sample Listings

Some of the top categories and sample charities on these sites are (and please keep in mind that these are listed as a small example of the kinds of charities you'll find—and should check out—on these sites):

Children's Charities

- Child Welfare League of America
- Children International

Community Development

- ACCION International
- City Cares
- The Empowerment Group

Education

- Braille Institute
- First Book (provides free, new books for low-income children)
- National Center for Family Literacy
- Reading is Fundamental

Environment

- Earth Conservation Corps
- Rainforest Alliance

Health

- Action Against Hunger
- The Alzheimer's Association
- Doctors Without Borders
- Gilda's Club
- Leukemia and Lymphoma Society

Social Justice

- Human Rights Watch

Hunger and Poverty

- Habitat for Humanity International
- Helen Keller Worldwide

Crime Prevention

- Center for the Prevention of Sexual and Domestic Violence

Arts and Culture

- American Center for Wine, Food and the Arts

Disabled

- Easter Seals
- Special Olympics International

Disaster Relief

- American National Red Cross
- Farm Aid

Sports and Recreation

- Big Brothers/Big Sisters of America
- Fresh Air Fund

Another added benefit to all the good you're doing with a charitable registry setup to benefit a cause you believe in is that these sites often *invite* you to suggest additional nonprofits for them to assess and possibly add to their registry option list. If you believe enough in a certain charity, and that charity meets the high standards of ethical behavior and legitimacy when the sites do a thorough search on them, *you* could be the catalyst for hundreds of thousands of dollars donated to them in the future. Now *that's* the definition of "giving back!"

Why Stop There?

Inspired by the altruistic nature of charitable giving, you might wish to find even more ways to incorporate a sense of generosity into your wedding day. Visit www.MarriedForGood.com for smart ideas and links to sites that will accept your donations:

- **Second Harvest** A directory of local food banks that will accept all those leftovers after your reception and rehearsal dinner.

- **The Hospital Directory** Where you'll find local hospitals that are happy to accept your floral décor and centerpieces to brighten up their patients' rooms, waiting rooms, and common areas.

- **CareScout** Where you'll find listings of local nursing homes where your wedding-day flowers will brighten residents' days.

- **The National Coalition Against Domestic Violence** Where you'll find hotline numbers for information on how to donate your wedding day leftovers—food, flowers, favors, even your leftover cake—to women's and children's shelters and safe houses. Volunteers will likely come pick up your donation.

- And also the **Glass Slipper Project** (in Chicago) and **Operation Fairy Dust** (in New York City), which will accept donations of formal gowns and accessories for disadvantaged girls to wear to their proms. Both bridesmaids and very stylish moms of brides and grooms just love being able to donate their dresses to these organizations.

- You'll find a lot more in charitable giving on sites like this one, including a crowd favorite where the donation is a gift of your *time* rather than money. Check out VolunteerMatch. com for zip code–located volunteer opportunities in your area, and plan for a day helping out at a charity 5K race or painting and gardening at a Habitat for Humanity house instead of having a traditional bachelorette's party.

It's a wonderful thing that there's no shortage of places to give from the heart.

Your List of Charities That You Wish to Support

1. _____

2. _____

3. _____

4. _____

5. _____

6. _____

7. _____

8. _____

9. _____

10. _____

Chapter 38

Independent Registries

Plenty of independent stores and sites run their own registries. Some may be in-store only, and others are accessible through their Web sites. So, that means your guests from Portland could "shop" in your favorite little Maryland art boutique, having the gift sent to your house. This innovation in registries is on the rise, so be sure to check your local boutiques and stores to see if they have a registry in place. If not, suggest it! The trend is growing, and will continue to grow, since more and more couples love the idea of registering for unique items, some one-of-a-kind (like them!).

Here are a few of the most unique and exciting independent registries I've found:

Insperience Studio
3232 Peachtree Road NE
Atlanta, GA
404-814-8232
www.insperiencestudio.com

Walking into Insperience is . . . well, an *experience*. You'll see fully stocked kitchen settings billed as "lifestyle vignettes" designed with the latest products and home design ideas from top names like Whirlpool and KitchenAid. But this is not just any kitchen setup. Insperience lines up hard-to-find items like stand-up mixers in (get this) thirty-six colors. Chefs offer cooking classes and demonstrations on a regular basis, and even laundry room setups come with their own educational product training programs.

It's the way the products are displayed that makes this shop a unique registry. Unlike superstores where kitchen appliances are piled to the rafters and loaded in the aisles, this space functions more like a working home where you can choose your items from a professionally decorated layout. For all areas in your home and garden, you'll find their products broken down into the following self-described categories:

- **Relax.** As you might expect, these are the products that allow you to bliss out: bath and home spa products.
- **Relate.** Items chosen specifically for the role they play in your personal relationships, with each other, with family, friends, guests, and kids. That means specialty picture frames, home games, and other items you'll use during quality time spent with your loved ones.
- **Share.** This area relates to the way you share your home. That means cooking, having dinner parties, hosting special events at your place, having a glass of wine out on your terrace. You'll find unique hand-painted dishes and serveware, vases, pitchers, serving platters, unusual and noteworthy recipe boxes and recipe cards (perfect for sharing your favorite family dishes), specialty cookbooks, and wine accessories.
- **Take Care.** Making maintenance fun, this section focuses on specialty items, cleaners, and tools for taking care of your appliances and your home. You'll find "I didn't know that existed" products like microwave cleaners, special cleaners for stainless steel, non-allergenic detergents, and specialty laundry accessories. All unique items you didn't know you needed but will be *very* happy to have on your list.

Insperience Studio says that the number one item on their brides' and grooms' wedding registries is the KitchenAid stand-up mixer, and this store offers the popular mixer in colors you won't find in department stores. Even more, the store offers the complete KitchenAid lineup of kitchen appliances—blenders, toasters, bakeware, kitchen gadgets, and other items—in the same hard-to-find-elsewhere colors.

Karen Kelsh, retail operations manager for Insperience Studio, sums up the allure of the independent store that's smart enough to establish its own unique and creative bridal registry: "Our goal . . . is to offer a pleasant and interactive experience for the guest. Plus, we hope to show them something they might not see anywhere else in Atlanta."

Maxwell Silver

New York, NY
212-799-1711
www.maxwellsilverny.com

Vogue and *W* magazines called this registry "chic," referring to its original, hip wedding gifts right from the heart of its main Soho location in New York City. The most unique angle of this registry is that it encompasses a number of boutiques in the city, allowing shopping access to a wide range of trendy and one-of-a-kind "finds" all over the Big Apple.

You can register online or in-store with the help of a registry consultant, or over the phone and through e-mail if you're outside the city and still want the consultant's help. You can even arrange for the consultant to e-mail you photos of the items you're looking for: you describe your style, and your own "personal shopper" hunts it down for you. While some fees may apply to certain services, city-chic brides and grooms love the experience of downloading a map to their member boutiques and hitting the pavement to scout them out in person.

This company's motto is "You aren't ordinary . . . why should your home be?" So for an extraordinary registry experience, this store and site could be the find of a lifetime.

Graziella, Ltd.

203 Pierce Street
Birmingham, MI
248-723-5650

This small, upscale retail store sells china, crystal, silver, and linens—much of which is imported from Europe and is therefore unlike most choices available in department stores. Their smaller scale and personalized registry consultant service makes for a much more focused assistance experience and a more private shopping spree among items you won't find anywhere else.

Where to Find Independent Registries Near You

Just pick up a copy of your state or city's bridal magazine, or a version such as *Modern Bride Connections*, which has regional versions for a wide range of cities across the country. In these, articles and resource lists will guide you right to those wonderful little boutiques and state-of-the-art stores you never knew were in your area. For example, I picked up a copy of *New York Weddings*, a special issue produced by *New York* magazine, and found a few dozen unique registries from the artsy to the exorbitant. Some examples in the New York City area that this issue pointed me toward:

- **Armani Casa.** Yes, it's *that* Armani, featuring contemporary items for the home, www.armanicasa.com
- **Avventura.** High-end tableware from the lines of Deruta and Moretti, very chic, www.forthatspecialgift.com
- **Baccarat.** Everything crystal, www.baccarat.com
- **Bridge Kitchenware.** Pro-quality kitchenware and small appliances, also shopped at by professional chefs, www.bridgekitchenware.com
- **Ceramica.** Hand-painted Italian ceramic plates and bowls, www.ceramicadirect.com
- **Clio.** Unusual home décor items, tableware, linens, and more from around the world, www.clio-home.com
- **Frette.** Upscale, ultra-luxurious bath and bedroom linens, www.frette.com
- **Harvey Electronics.** A mecca for top-quality plasma television sets, digital media players, high definition TVs, and home theater equipment, www.harveyelectronics.com
- **Zabars.** A mecca for kitchen gadgets, www.zabars.com

These are just *some* of the unique registries in the New York City area. You'll find plenty where you live, scouting through bridal magazines and your city's wedding Web sites (like www.njwedding.com, www.chicagobride.com, www.rhodeislandbride.com, and others) for listings you can scout on your own.

Unique Registries

They're just starting to bloom, but you will find a wide range of unique independent registries popping up all over the place, with smart companies and services offering bridal registries as a way for brides and grooms to enhance their lifestyles and well-being through their wedding gifts. Check out the following categories and look for such registries in your area:

- Bottled spring water delivery services
- Buy-a-car programs: like a honeymoon registry, only you're registering for a car with all the accessories and options
- Country club memberships
- Day spa gift certificates (imagine loading up here!!)
- Dining programs, special clubs that give you member cards to earn points and get discounts at participating restaurants
- Farm co-ops
- Gardening shops
- Gym memberships
- Housecleaning services
- Landscaping services, including winter plowing
- Lingerie salons
- Massage appointments
- Membership to a swim club or the town swimming pool
- Organic food stores and co-ops
- Pet supply stores
- Pool and hot tub stores
- Pool cleaning services

- Private golf course memberships
- Rounds of golf at premiere courses
- Sporting goods stores and ski shops
- Theater tickets, such as a membership to a local community theater for season-long discount tickets and special VIP galas
- Tuition to educational courses, such as advanced degrees and professional certificates
- Tuition to workshops, both personal and business
- Yoga studio memberships

Organic Wedding Registries

I saved this one for last, with the caveat that it is not an independent registry, but rather a partnership between several different online sites. OrganicWeddings.com has long been recognized as a wonderful site for buying natural and earth-friendly items, and now in partnership with Felicite.com (you read about them back in Books and Music), this site brings you right to an organic bridal registry setup at a site called Greenfeet.com (it's less confusing than it sounds!).

Here you can sign up for an incredibly vast range of home products, all organic and natural. Today's couples who live by organic standards and the wish for clean air and environmentally sound processes *love* having this option now. While you can certainly find some organic items on other Web sites, this registry offers nothing but.

Among the items you'll find at the bridal registry of Organic Weddings.com/Greenfeet.com:

- A hammock made from 100 percent organic materials
- A recycled fleece fluffy "bean bag" chair
- Air purifiers
- Energy-efficient appliances
- Essential oils and diffusers
- Hemp rugs, bags, and other items
- Lavender spa products like booties, mittens, eye pillows, heat wraps, and neck pillows
- Mattress pads made from natural fibers
- Natural soaps and hair-care products

- Organic bedsheets and mattresses made from an organic cotton/wool blend
- Organic cotton robes
- Organic cotton towels
- Organic home cleaning products
- Organic laundry detergents and fabric softeners, lavender linen water (*love* this product for great-smelling sheets and towels!) and closet sachets
- Organic lavender sachets and aromatherapy products
- Pillows made with natural and recycled fibers, beans, or organic buckwheat
- Recycled glass home décor items
- Water conservation systems
- Zen gardens and miniature gardens
- And more . . .

If you share a mutual love of all things organic, this could be your ideal bridal registry site.

Couples with Kids

Engaged couples who have kids from previous relationships, and are thus blending their families into one, are sliding a few family-style items onto their wedding registries, such as Sony PlayStations and Xbox games ("Seriously, it's for me! Really!") and the appropriate games and accessories, kids' bedding sets (so that both daughters' comforters match in their new, shared bedroom), cases of snacks and bottled water service, kids' toys for the backyard party oasis, bean bag chairs, artwork and lamps that are really for the kids' rooms ("Seriously, we *love* the purple curvy balloon lights!"), oversized beach towels, CD players and DVD players for the family room, security system for the home (of course), sleeping bags, mountain bikes, and other fun items.

Cashing in on what Mom and Dad register for could make the whole blending families transition a little bit easier for the kids!

The Strangest Thing on Our List

Intrigued by the originality of these registries, and the creativity used within traditional registries, I asked brides and grooms across the country for the strangest and most surprising items they included on their registries. Here's what they said:

"Paper products—we registered for cases of paper towels, toilet paper, and napkins, which we now have stored in bulk down in our basement. Works like a charm."

"Cleaning products, like rust removers, stain removers, disinfectant sprays, and others."

"Lavender-scented laundry water, to add in and make our sheets smell terrific."

"Burt's Bees foot cream."

"Contact lens solution."

"Shammies for cleaning our car."

"A barbecue grill *flosser*. Don't laugh, it's going to be very popular someday! It cleans out the spaces between the grill lines, where the brushes can't get."

"Cases of Little Debbie snacks and Cracker Jacks . . . we go to professional football games every weekend, and we bring these as snacks at the game."

"Socks. Really warm, scrunchy socks to keep my feet warm in winter."

"A dry-erase board for the refrigerator front so that I can just write down all the jobs he has to do around the house."

"We have lots of pets—four dogs, three cats, a bird, and a rabbit—so we registered for new dog beds and pet supplies. Hey, we need that kind of stuff!"

"Well, we thought about putting down birth control supplies, but we didn't think our mothers would like that very much ☺."

Chapter 39

Real Couples Say . . .

This chapter comes right to you from real couples—newly engageds and longtime-marrieds—with their stories about their bridal registries. The first part is a collection of the coolest and most extravagant things today's brides- and grooms-to-be have placed on their bridal registries.

The second, perhaps even more inspiring, shares those items that have stood the test of time, the one or two wedding gifts the couple received all those years ago that they *still* treasure, the most enduring wedding gifts they own.

Today's New Couples: What's Hot on Our List

"Our top gift has to be our sheet and towel sets. We'll use them every day, and they just came as a gift from a friend's mother—who wasn't even on our wedding guest list. It was a very generous and thoughtful gift from her." —Denise and Andrew from California

"We registered for a sound system, and the other item we registered for and received is a curio cabinet. I love it, love it, love it!" —Lisa and John from New Jersey

"A scone pan from Williams-Sonoma" —Diana and Larry from Pennsylvania

A Choice for a Cause

"A unique item we put on our registry was the Williams-Sonoma KitchenAid Artisan Stand Mixer in pink. When you purchase this pink Artisan mixer, KitchenAid will donate $50 to the Susan G. Komen Breast Cancer Foundation as part of their Cook for the Cure initiative. My grandmother (a breast cancer survivor) not only purchased my favorite gift on the registry, but she also supported a great cause! Every time I use the pink mixer I will think of her!" —Carey and Joshua from New Jersey

"An underwater dive camera and dive watch—and we got the camera ☺ " —Michelle and Michael in New York

"A heated mattress pad." —Elizabeth and Patrick in New Jersey

"The most unique and useful item would be space bags, which condense clothing/blankets, etc. when you vacuum out the air for easy storage. We already have a house and mostly everything for it, and also a three-year-old daughter with a lot of baby clothes to put away. They are great for seasonal clothes also." —Toni and James in New Jersey

"Camping equipment—tents, lanterns, coolers, chairs, gas camping stove. Wood towel holder, free standing outdoors. Chainsaw and skill saw." —Kathy and Richard from Pennsylvania

The Wildest Thing We Registered For

"An authentic Ms. Pacman and Galaga arcade game from Fortunoff. It's $3,000 so we don't expect anyone to buy it, but we had to put it on anyway because you never know!" —Beth and Adam from New Jersey

Longtime Marrieds: What's Lasted So Long

"It sounds mundane, but the one item we received ten years ago that we still use all the time is our salad spinner. We had a Crate and Barrel registry, and it's been my most used item." —Barbara in California

"I've been married twice, and the first gift that popped into my mind for this question is a clear glass bowl about the size of a salad plate. It has a divider and came with a pickle fork. I've used it for countless parties over the past forty years, using it to serve pickles, olives, relishes, mints and nuts, candies, you name it. Nearly every time I have company, that bowl comes out for one reason or another." —Charlene Ann, owner of www.dontmissyourlife.com

"The gift we love and use daily is a great set of knives from Wustof Trident that my brother-in-law and his wife gave us. My husband Charlie and I have been married for six years." —Marcia in New York

"Our china pattern. We've used it for all kinds of family parties over the years, and we'll use it again for my daughter's bridal shower next month." — Claire in Boston

"Our fireplace set—it's one of those things that you don't even realize makes such a difference in your home. We've spent many winter nights sitting by that fireplace, reading, playing games as a family, and entertaining our guests." —Lila and Jim from Ontario

"Our bedroom lamps. We've gotten new shades for them over the years, but they're the most lasting thing we received, and they're still so beautiful and classic." — Maureen and Tom from San Antonio

"A set of candlestick holders, shaped like roses and made out of crystal. We put them out for all of our holiday dinners, family parties, and for romantic dinners just for the two of us." —Dana and Ed from Aspen

"A red throw blanket that we keep on the arm of our couch. It's so soft, worn softer by age, and it's our kids' favorite blanket to snuggle up under. It has stains on it, some bleach marks, and the edging is frayed, but that's from a lot of years of good use." —Elaine and Serge from Miami

Part Six

AFTER THE WEDDING

Chapter 40

Use It All Year

A fter your wedding date, your bridal registry account will most often remain active and online for up to a year. And on some sites, the items left over on your pre–wedding list can be bought at a discount. That means your bridal registry can be used for your upcoming birthday gifts (both yours and his), for holiday gifts, anniversaries, Valentine's Day, graduations, and other gift-giving events.

Suggest that close friends and family shop for you off of your registry list—which they might not be aware of as an option for your birthday or the winter holidays. They'll be happy to find the ease of ordering and delivery right to you, and also a guarantee that they're getting you things you still want and need. It's a win-win for both of you.

Renew your Wedding Web Site

You can purchase an extended subscription to your personalized wedding Web site—complete with links to your bridal registry—to match that one year your registry remains active after the big day. Check out renewal subscriptions (such as at www.wedstudio.com) so that your friends and family can easily find your registry online later on.

The two of you could agree to shop off the registry list for your own upcoming birthdays, any special anniversaries you celebrate (like the eighth anniversary of your first date, in case you're keeping track), holiday gifts, and even those special little romantic surprise gifts you're always giving to one another.

One big category for after-wedding registry shopping is your housewarming party. Especially if your home downpayment registry has put you over the top, and you've bought your first house, what better source than your bridal registry for those housewarming gifts your parents, relatives, and friends will surely bring to your place? Sure, you always have the option of setting up a separate gift registry for that—and might choose to do so—but don't forget that items you buy from your own bridal registry might be steeply discounted for you.

Chapter 41

Say Thank You

Your guests have given you wonderful things, the items to fill your home and create your lifestyle together. Now it's time for you to say thank you with a wonderful expression of your gratitude.

You already know that sending thank-you notes is an unbreakable rule, and the long-standing rules of etiquette state that a handwritten note is a *must*. While some couples are bending this rule to send cute, animated thank-yous online to their Internet-connected friends, the vast majority are sticking to handwritten thank-yous, complete with a copy of their wedding day portrait tucked into each.

You can order gorgeous thank-you notes personalized with your monogram, or you can purchase attractive blank thank-you notes at a stationery store. The design is up to you. Some couples match their thank-you note ensemble to their wedding invitations, ordering them as part of their invitation set; others choose their thank-yous according to their wedding's theme . . . such as a beige card with a great line drawing of the beach, sand dunes, and a sunset. Something reminiscent of the beautiful wedding you all shared.

You have plenty of freedom in your thank-you note design, and that freedom also extends to what you write inside the card. The most gracious and classy couples out there personalize their messages to each recipient. That means no "Thanks for the wedding gift!" scrawled in your very tired handwriting, and no computer-printed mass-produced general message on each card. You can't just hit "print" on your home computer and whip out a hundred thank-you notes without picking up a pen. This is one area where hi-tech efficiency doesn't apply.

Each of your thank-you notes needs to be written out by hand.

Personalizing Your Thank-You Notes

The Top Tips for Creating Lovely and Heartfelt Thank-Yous

- Thank the givers by name inside the card (as in "Dear George, Anna, and Annamarie")

- Mention the specific gift they gave you, and tell them how much you love the item they chose for you. Get detailed, as in "We love the bud vases so much—we have them on our kitchen windowsill, and Mike has been surprising me each morning with fresh cuttings from our garden. Our kitchen smells so wonderful, and it's a great way to start off our day." Guests *love* to hear how the gift they chose for you makes your day brighter, how you use it in your home, and even compliments you're getting from others on it (as in "Thank you so much for the gorgeous red platter. Everyone who comes to our place loves it, and they've been asking us where we got it! We say 'We have friends with terrific taste!' That color makes our entire room light up."). Nothing makes a wedding guest feel better than knowing you really do love what they chose for you, and their egos get a boost when others admire their choice as well. You will make their day.

- If a guest has given you a gift card, let them know what you purchased with it. "Dear Maya and Henry, Thank you so much for your generous gift. We had such a blast going to the store to pick out our new coffeemaker! And we also got a set of beautiful footed coffee mugs we love so much. Thanks!"

- If you've received a group gift, something big-ticket that all of your work friends or all of the groomsmen gave you, be sure to send each individual within the group his or her own thank-you note. Very important: Make sure you're clear on exactly who is included in the "group," so that you won't leave anyone out with your thank-yous. If all of their names are on the card attached to the gift, individually signed with little messages to you, this job will be easier. If not, if the card is signed "The Girls from the Office," then you need to check with *two* trusted people within the group to get the names of who actually joined in on the present. I say "check with two" because you don't want to take the chance of one person not being complete with his or her list. Checking with two sources will help you create the full list. It's just good protocol.

- Pay special homage to gift-givers who went above and beyond. If your boss's gift of a $200 bottle of wine made your jaw drop, be sure to thank her with a handwritten note of sincere gratitude, and the added detail that you both will drink a toast to your boss when you open that bottle on the day you move into your new home. Your boss is a person, too, a generous person, and we all love hearing a genuine thank-you. We all love knowing the added sentimentality we gave to someone.

- If you plan to include a copy of your wedding portrait in each thank-you note, be sure you have enough portraits for all of your guests! I've seen cringe-worthy faux pas where couples included their small wedding portrait in notes to the "bigger benefactors," the people who gave terrific, expensive gifts, but then not enclose a portrait in cards to "the little people," those whose $25 gifts didn't impress. This isn't a class or caste system. All of your guests, in all of their different budget categories, came to your wedding and gave you gifts from their hearts. Classifying them by who gets a photo of you and who doesn't is a bad move. People talk, and feelings get hurt when friends are discussing your wedding photo to a friend who didn't get one. That's a sour aftertaste after all that friend did to attend your wedding.

- Think about sending a different kind of photo besides your official wedding couple portrait taken by your photographer. You could send a terrific picture of the two of you on a blanket, snuggling in front a beachside sunset, with your wedding rings prominently displayed. With digital cameras and the supremely inexpensive developing fees at sites like www.ofoto.com, you can order as many prints as you need for far, far less than ordering them professionally.

- Consider tailoring your thank-you note photo to incorporate something the guest gave you as a wedding gift. Again, use your digital camera on timer to snap a shot of the two of you wearing those plush spa robes during your honeymoon, and then send that picture to the guest who gave you those robes. How terrific that their gift became a part of your most romantic trip of a lifetime! For guests who kicked into your honeymoon registry, send them an underwater picture of the two of you scuba diving, or a great shot of you standing next to a tropical waterfall. For guests who contributed to your home downpayment fund, include a picture of your new husband carrying you across the threshold. Your friends and families love receiving these personalized photos of you. In fact, they're far more likely to display them in their homes or offices when it's a more casual picture like that than an official, posed wedding couple portrait in gown and tux.

- Send the official wedding couple gown and tux portraits to parents, grandparents, siblings, and the bridal party—those you feel should have the more official photo. As fun as your friends would find the scuba diving picture in your thank-you note, your grandmother might be offended at your lack of decorum. Judge according to each recipient.

- Create your own attractive thank-you notes on your home computer, printing a great color graphic of the two of you on the cover, with your handwritten note inside. Use matte or glossy greeting card stock from an office supply store to make the look as professional as possible.

- Add a little accent to your thank-you notes, such as a mono-grammed foil seal on the back of your envelope, or use the rest of those Love stamps you bought for your wedding invitations.

- Include your new business card or an at-home card in this thank-you packet, if you wish. Your guests can take this small card with all of your new contact information (and your name change status, if applicable) and attach it right into their address books.

- If you're sending a thank-you to a parent's friends, or some-one who attended your wedding but you're not particularly familiar with, be sure to add your last name when you sign the thank-you note. They'll identify you more easily that way.

- If, say, a friend of yours brought a date to your wedding and the gift was from both of them together, be sure to thank them both by name in the card, even if that date was a stranger to you.

Faux Pas Alert!

Be sure to get the correct guest's name off their wedding card, especially if your friend switched dates at the last minute. Don't automatically rely on your invitation list, as your friend could be on his third girlfriend since you invited him.

- Double-check that your chosen shape and size of thank-you note doesn't need extra postage. Some sizes (and shapes like squares) require a second stamp per envelope. Just like with your wedding invitations, you wouldn't want to waste time, money, and effort when *all* of your thank-yous come back to you with that big, ugly "Returned for Postage" stamp on it. That means buying and writing out all new envelopes.

- And finally, use a terrific pen. At the office supply store, you'll find calligraphy felt pens, colorful gel pens, even metallic silver or copper pens. Depending on your style of thank-you, this added design touch could make your thank-you notes extra special.

Sitting Down to Write Thank-You Notes

- Make it an event, something to look forward to rather than dreading. Plan a special breakfast or dinner for the two of you—enjoy your wedding gifts while preparing and serving it—and follow up by digging into your thank-you note writing session. Come up with the wording of your messages together, to tailor each note and add special meaning. It's terrific these days when the groom adds his own message to the thank-you card.

- Speaking of your groom, you both should sign the thank-you notes. Sure, you could sign for both of you, but the groom gets extra points for giving his autograph as well.

- If you don't have time to write out 200 thank-you notes in one sitting, break it down into chunks: 50 today, 50 this weekend, and so on.

- Don't stall in planning this thank-you note session. Get to it as soon as possible, since procrastination only gets harder to overcome with time. Brides and grooms of the past often had to wait weeks if not months for their wallet-size wedding portraits to come back from the photographer, and *then* they could do their thank-you notes. Now, you have less of a cushion. With digital proofs and streamlined development processes often returning your wedding picture package in a week or so, you can get right on it.

Note from the Author

NOW THAT YOU'VE BEEN INSPIRED, now that you've started thinking beyond your original wedding registry wish list, it's time for you to embark on one of the most enjoyable planning sessions possible. Unlike with your actual wedding, no one is questioning your choices, pressuring you to choose the "proper" item, or inserting their wish list into your own. Your registry is yours, and yours alone, to plan the way you wish.

This is an indulgent time, so go for the best! Upgrade the items you own. Register for celebrity-style luxurious items. Go high-tech. Dress your rooms and your home with expressions of your personality and style, touched and given life by all of your most sentimental and valued belongings. This is your home to design and build choice by choice, your oasis from the world, the place where your married life will take root and grow.

I wish you all the best as you create your home and enjoy every moment to come. Thank you for allowing me to help you get started, and I invite you to send me your own wedding registry stories, the most luxurious item you registered for, the most surprising thing you or your groom registered for, and any other registry stories you'd like to share in future editions of this book. Visit me at www.sharonnaylor.net to submit your stories, and you could see your name in print in my next book.

Happy shopping, and a very happy future to both of you . . .

All the best,
Sharon Naylor

Appendix 1

Your Registry Locations

Category: _____

Store: _____

Web Site: _____

800 Number: _____

Registry ID Number: _____

Category: _____

Store: _____

Web Site: _____

800 Number: _____

Registry ID Number: _____

Category: _____

Store: _____

Web Site: _____

800 Number: _____

Registry ID Number: _____

Appendix 2

Upgrade List

Things We Want to Upgrade with Our Registry

1. _____

2. _____

3. _____

4. _____

5. _____

6. _____

7. _____

8. _____

9. _____

10. _____

11. _____

12. _____

13. _____

14. _____

15. _____

Appendix 3

Our Wished-For Group Gifts

1. _____
2. _____
3. _____
4. _____
5. _____
6. _____
7. _____
8. _____
9. _____
10. _____
11. _____
12. _____
13. _____
14. _____
15. _____

Resources

Wedding Web Sites

The Best Man: www.thebestman.com
The Big Day: www.thebigday.com
Bliss Weddings: www.blissweddings.com
Bride's Magazine: www.brides.com
Della Weddings: www.dellaweddings.com
Elegant Bride: www.elegantbridemagazine.com
The Knot: www.theknot.com
Martha Stewart Living: www.marthastewart.com
Modern Bride: www.ModernBride.com
Premiere Bride: www.premierebride.com
Today's Bride: www.todaysbride.com
Town and Country Weddings (upscale): www.tncweddings.com
Wedding Bells: www.weddingbells.com
Wedding Central: www.weddingcentral.com
The Wedding Channel: www.theweddingchannel.com
Wedding Details: www.weddingdetails.com

Wedding Registries

Barneys: 888-BARNEYS[227-6397], www.barneys.com
Bed Bath & Beyond: 800-GO-BEYOND[462-3966],
    www.bedbathandbeyond.com
The Big Day: 800-304-1141, www.thebigday.com
Bloomingdales: 888-269-3187, www.bloomingdales.com
Bon Ton: 800-9BONTON[926-6866], www.bonton.com
Crate & Barrel: 800-967-6696, www.crateandbarrel.com
Cruise Direct Online (cruises): 800-365-1445,
    www.cruisedirect.com

Dillards: 800-345-5273, www.dillards.com

Felicite: www.felicite.com

Filene's: 800-9-SAY-I-DO[972-9436], www.FilenesWeddings.com

Fortunoff: 800-FORTUNOFF[367-8866], www.fortunoff.com

Go Celebrate: 877-933-0003, store.gocelebrate.com

Greenfeet (organic bridal registry): 888-5-NATURE[562-8873], www.greenfeet.com (access also through www.organicweddings.com)

Gump's: 800-444-0450, www.gumps.com

Hecht's: 800-9-SAY-I-DO[972-9436], www.hechts.com

Home Depot: 800-553-3199, www.homedepot.com (Registries are handled online—as of this writing, Home Depot did not have in-store registry kiosks.)

HoneyLuna (honeymoon registry): 800-809-LUNA[5862], www.honeyluna.com

The Honeymoon (honeymoon registry): 888-796-7772, www.thehoneymoon.com

JCPenney: 800-322-1189, www.jcpgift.com

Just Give: 866-587-8448 www.justgive.org

Kohl's: 866-887-8884, www.kohls.com

Linens-n-Things: 866-568-7378, www.lnt.com

Macy's Wedding Channel: 888-92-BRIDES[922-7433], www.macys.weddingchannel.com

Neiman Marcus: 888-888-4757, www.neimanmarcus.com

Pier 1 Imports: 800-245-4595, www.pier1.com

Pottery Barn: 888-779-5176, www.potterybarn.com

REI (outdoor and camping): 800-426-4840, www.rei.com

Restoration Hardware: 800-762-1005, www.restorationhardware.com

Saks Fifth Avenue: 800-331-6552, www.saksfifthavenue.com

Sears: 800-349-4358, www.sears.com

Service Merchandise: 866-978-2583, www.servicemerchandise.com

Sharper Image: 800-344-5555, www.sharperimage.com

Starwood Honeymoon Registry: 800-503-7800,
   www.weddingchannel.com

Sur La Table: 800-243-0852, www.surlatable.com

Target's Club Wedd Gift Registry: 800-888-9333,
   www.target.com

Tiffany & Co.: 800-843-3269, www.tiffany.com

Wedding Channel.com: www.weddingchannel.com

Williams-Sonoma: 877-812-6235, www.williams-sonoma.com

Glossary

WHAT'S THE DIFFERENCE between Supima cotton and combed cotton? Give up? Here, you'll find definitions for many of the terms you may encounter as you put together your bridal registry.

Fabrics

Acrylic   A soft synthetic fiber, used most often in blankets.

Anchor band pad   A mattress pad that covers just the top of the mattress, secured around the four corners of the mattress by elastic holders.

Baffling   A form of sewing down comforters in which cloth sections, rather than simple stitching, keeps the down segments in place. This is considered the finest form of comforter construction.

Bath linens   "Linens" is an encompassing term for all of the fabric items used in your bathroom—towels, washcloths, face towels, rugs, bath mats, and more.

Bath sheet   An oversized bath towel, most often 36 by 72 inches or 30 by 60 inches.

Bath towel   A standard size towel

Bed linens   Just like with the bathroom, this term rounds up your sheets, blankets, duvet covers, pillowcases, shams, quilts, bed skirts, decorative pillows, and canopies.

Bed skirt   A fitting or wrap of decorative fabric to match or compliment your comforter and bedding. Fits over the boxspring of your bed and hangs down to the floor.

Blouson valance   A form of valance in which the construction of fabric allows for it to be stuffed (and thus puffy) or left to hang straight.

Canopy   A soft, wispy hanging of fabric from the ceiling or from a post bed to surround the bed with fabric or netting.

Construction   The stitch pattern in sheets and comforters. Open construction is a form where the top and bottom layers are stitched together in a wider pattern, allowing the down or fill to move about. Closed construction is a more patterned form of stitching bottom and top together into squares or patterns that keep down or fill more in place. Baffled construction is a detailed stitch pattern that allows optimum movement of down or fill, making it most expensive.

Cotton A primary material for bedding, bath towels, and other home furnishings, this fabric is soft and breathable. The main categories of cotton are the following:

- *Egyptian*—A super-fine cotton from Egypt, among the most popular and most requested, the most luxurious according to style experts.
- *American Upland cotton*—A basic, popular cotton most often used in home bedding and furnishings.
- *Pima cotton*—A top cotton choice for its soft touch, popular for bedding sets and towels, often called the American version of Egyptian cotton.
- *Supima cotton*—Extra-long cotton fibers make up this soft version for sheets and towels.
- *Sea Island cotton*—A highly luxurious blend of cotton, considered among the best on the market.
- *Combed cotton*—A form of cotton construction that removes the shorter fibers, leaving the longest fibers (in a "combing" process) for a soft finish.
- *100 percent cotton*—A top choice for the quality of feel, may shrink a bit if not pretreated, many couples prefer this to blends.
- *Cotton-poly blend*—Usually 50-50 blends of cotton and polyester. This blend is known for being more wrinkle-resistant than pure cotton, but is not as soft or breathable.

Down The material used to fill comforters and pillows, most often feathers from geese or ducks, also a synthetic down as a possibility.

Down alternative The name for comforter or pillow fillers that is not authentic bird down, but rather a substitution or synthetic fiber.

Drapery panels The lengths of fabric hung from curtain rods as part of the window treatment. Usually found in lengths of 63, 84 (the most common), and 96 inches, but available in other sizes as well.

Dust ruffle   A fabric arrangement that hangs from the bed frame to the floor, extending the bedding ensemble's look in completion. Also called a "bed skirt."

Duvet cover   A slipcover for a comforter to slide into, stitched on three sides, and closed with buttons on the open side.

Embellished towel   A decorative towel with add-on embroidery or lace appliques, for display only.

Fill power   Related to down comforters, this is the quality rating of materials used to fill the comforter. The larger the down material, the higher the fill power. The 550–650 fill power is considered ideal.

Fingertip towel   A small towel measuring in at 11 by 18 inches or 12 by 20 inches for hand-drying, or for décor. Some styles may have lace or applique embellishments as well.

Flannel   A soft, thicker and cozy fabric, most often used in colder weather for sheets and blankets.

Jacquard   A weave of different-colored threads creates this fabric design.

Knit   A soft cotton version, often seen in T-shirt or jersey styles for bedding.

Muslin   A frequent choice for sheets and slipcovers, muslin is a woven form of fabric.

Olefin   A fabric most often used in sofas, slipcovers, and curtains, known for its high durability and light weight.

Oxford   A heavier form of fabric, soft enough for bedsheets.

Percale   A finely woven bed linen, known for its ease of care.

Pilling (or **Pills**)   Small frayed gatherings of fabric that form over time in lower thread count cotton blends. Some fabrics will be marketed as "pill-resistant" and you will find pill-remover tools to "shave" pills from fabrics, comforters, and pillows.

Pinpoint   The top level of percale sheets, with a higher thread count (220–250, on the average).

Pinpoint Weave   A softer form of weave, this construction is made with two stitches over and one stitch under for a durable blend with notable smoothness.

Poly-cluster   A form of pillow made with silicone-covered polyester clusters, among the most supportive synthetic pillows.

Print towel   A design of towel in which the design is printed or stamped onto the fabric.

Sanforized   A pre-shrinking process for sheets.

Sateen   A higher thread count cotton, very soft and luxurious.

Sateen weave   Among the softest weaves, this form is made with four stitches over and one stitch under, providing more stitches on the surface of the fabric.

Sham   A large decorative bedding pillow.

Slipcover   A construction of fabric designed to slip over couches or chairs for a new color, pattern, and fabric cover. Edges are tucked in to create a smooth look.

Synthetic fibers   Any fiber that is man-made, such as acrylic or polyester.

Table linens   The category for your tablecloths, napkins, table runners, placemats, and other fabric used on the table.

Terry   A soft and absorbent fabric most often used for towels and robes, this fabric is made of smooth uncut loops of cotton construction.

Thermal weave   A loosely woven creation used most often in thermal blankets.

Thread count   The number of threads per square inch of fabric. The higher the number, the softer and more luxurious the fabric. The ideal is 400-count, but you'll see numbers higher than that—and pay for it too! FYI in case you're on *Jeopardy* any time soon: the term for the lengthwise threads is the "warp," and the widthwise is the "weft."

Towel Weight   The thickness and weight of a towel, which determines its price.

Vellux   A nylon and foam blend creating a thick and soft synthetic fabric.

Velour   The fiber loops have been cut in this fabric, creating a soft but not optimally absorbent fabric for towels.

Washcloth   Nine- to thirteen-inch squares of cloth for washing.

Wool   A thick, durable fabric providing lots of warmth and great insulation.

Wrap mattress pad   A full mattress pad that slips on like a fitted sheet, with elastic that secures its position at the bottom of the mattress. Often quilted on the top and sides.

Window Treatments

Café rods A decorative curtain rod that comes in a range of $^1/_2$- to $^3/_4$-inch thickness.

Combination rods A combination of a single curtain and Dauphine rod in one, this treatment is used to hang sheers and drapes together or a valance and rod pocket panel together.

Decorative curtain rods Made of either wood or metal, these curtain rods may be fitted with finials or be created with grooves or structure for greater décor accenting.

Finials Decorative end pieces on curtain rods, sometimes wood, metal, crystal, or theme-shaped accents.

Holdbacks Hooks or fabric loops attached to brackets that hold back curtain panels as part of a decorative or light-allowing arrangement in window treatments.

Magnetic curtain rods Used to attach curtain rods to steel doors using strong magnets.

Projection The measurement of space between the wall or window and the window treatment.

Sash rods Rods usually used on doors and French doors.

Scarf valance A length of fabric used as a decorative drape in and around window treatments. Sold in six-foot to eight-foot lengths and available in a wide range of fabrics, with or without beading and decorative accents.

Sconces Accessory used to hang scarf valances or hold curtain rods.

Single curtain rods Used with sheer or lace panels, these curtain rods are ideal for layering effects in window treatments.

Spring tension rods Round or oval curtain rods that attach with built-in spring tension to wall mounts for a secure hang.

Swag holders Accessory used to hold scarf valances in place.

Cookware

Aluminum A durable metal, somewhat thin, highly conductible, very popular for cookware and bakeware.

Anodized aluminum A thicker, more durable form of aluminum that is treated to prevent warping and uneven heat levels. Most often darker in color than regular aluminum, this form warms more quickly and evenly.

Bakeware   A roundup term to encompass all items used for baking, such as cookie sheets, mixing bowls, pie pans, muffin tins, bread tins, and more.

Black steel (also "blue steel")   A specially treated metal used to create cooking pans, known for its durability and its even heat distribution.

Cast iron   A staple among cookware, this heavy material makes for popular skillets and cookware since it heats up evenly and is known to add iron content to the foods you prepare in it. Cast-iron cookware may need to be treated (or "seasoned") for optimum use over time.

Conductible metals   Metals that distribute heat evenly and quickly, such as aluminum, anodized aluminum, and copper.

Cookware   A roundup classification term for all the cooking pots and pans you'll need—sauce pans, frying pans, skillets, and others—used on your stovetop or in the oven.

Copper   A top choice among professional chefs for its heat distribution and quick cooling—essential for dishes in which temperature control is crucial—copper cookware requires some care. Copper pots are often displayed in a kitchen, making them decorative as well as efficient.

Enameled cast iron   A form of treating cast-iron pots and pans with a layer of enamel, thus rendering it protected from corrosion, not needing treatment, and perfect for long-cook preparation.

Enameled steel   Another treated form of cookware, this type is coated with several layers of enamel and comes with a stainless steel rim. Also called "porcelain enamel."

Insulated aluminum   Two layers of aluminum separated by a pocket of air in between them, providing an ideal baking surface most often used for cookie sheets and pizza pans.

Nonstick   A top choice if you don't want to spend hours scrubbing or cleaning, special materials are used in the creation of cookware, bakeware, appliances, and utensils to make surfaces non-catching and easy to clean. Also used in healthier cooking, since you don't need to add a lot of oil or butter to get a nonstick finish to dishes.

Riveted handles   The sturdiest and most secure attachment of handles to pots and pans, in which rivets are attached permanently through the pan metal.

Screwed on handles   A less durable and reliable attachment of handles, in which plastic handles are attached to the outside of the pan only.

Stainless Steel   Extremely durable, this type of steel creates an ideal cooking surface when bonded to a base of copper or aluminum, as is often seen on the market.

Welded handles   An attachment of handles to pots and pans using welding. Not as secure as riveted handles.

Stemware

Crystal   A finer form of glass, due to the addition of red lead oxide. This form of stemware maintains a great clarity and shine and as such is a top choice for fine stemware. *See also* "Lead crystal."

Etching   A decorative embossing of crystal or glasses, done either by hand or by machine, to add decorative designs to the bowl, stem, or rim of a glass.

Frosting   Another decorative method to add design detail to glasses, this one can apply a glazed or "frosted" icy look to glass areas.

Glassware   A category that refers to all drinking glasses, including champagne flutes, wine glasses, tumblers, snifters, highballs, juice glasses, and martini glasses.

Lead crystal   Also known as full lead crystal, is one of the finest forms of crystal on the market. This form of glass, due to its creation method, is fragile and extremely valuable.

Stemware   The category for formal glassware, including wine glasses (red and white varieties), water goblets, champagne flutes, and martini glasses.

Tempered glass   A special treatment renders this type of glass stronger when dealing with extreme hot and extreme cold.

Glassware Details

Brandy snifter   Short-stemmed, this wide bowl glass is perfect for drinking brandy and other liqueurs (bartenders often fill them so that the drink would just touch the rim if the glass were laid on its side).

Champagne flute A narrow, stemmed glass perfect for drinking champagne and mimosas.

Cordial glass Also called a "sherry glass," this small glass resembles a shot glass or a miniature brandy snifter with a stem and wide footing.

Daiquiri glass Tall and on a long stem, this glass is wider for daiquiri servings.

Double old-fashioned Also known as "rocks" glasses, these short glasses with no stem—round, square, or octagonal—are often used for drinking hard liquor straight on the rocks.

Highball A taller glass used to serve mixed drinks.

Juice glass A small glass used for informal drinks, may be flat-based or footed.

Margarita glass This wide glass has a curved bowl for holding classic margaritas.

Martini glass A triangular glass on a stem, some wider or narrower than others.

Pilsner A tall, slender footed pint or beer glass.

Port glass Like a wine glass but smaller, with a more pointed bowl, for serving dessert wines.

Red wine glass A wine glass that is wider than the white wine glass, allowing more air to reach the surface of red wine for its optimal taste.

Shot glass A small glass with a flat base, or a rounded base for setting in ice chips.

Tilted A design in which the glass is created to look like it's leaning to the side.

Water goblet Stemmed and with a larger bowl than the red wine glass.

White wine glass The standard wine glass with a narrower bowl (or cup portion).

Flatware

Banded Cutlery or flatware that features an etched band around the handles.

Carbon steel A top level of metal for the creation of very sharp knives.

Cutlery   The classification for all things used to cut: kitchen knives, steak knives, kitchen shears, etc.

Electroplating   A method of creating flatware in which an electric current is used to adhere gold plating and silver plating to metal. This treatment is known to make flatware more durable and is a top choice.

Flat ground   A type of knife in which the blade is ground to a curved taper at the end.

Flatware   The category encompassing utensils for the tabletop. The usual five-piece place setting includes a dinner knife, dinner fork, salad fork, teaspoon, and tablespoon. The top varieties are sterling silver, silverplate, and stainless steel.

Forged blades   A form of knives in which the shape of the blade is hammered out of steel.

Gold plate   The result of electroplating in which a thin layer of 10-karat gold is applied to a flatware metal form, resulting in gold-plated utensils.

Hollow ground   Not as durable as flat ground blades, this form has a concave curve shape to it.

Laser-constructed   Serrated knives designed by computer and laser cut.

Luncheon size   This category of flatware is a smaller sized version of the average flatware setting.

Serrated   A scalloped design of the knife blade, making it perfect for cutting bread or bagels. Serrated knives come in fine or wider "teeth" for ease of use and cannot be sharpened.

Silver plate   The result of electroplating in which a layer of 100 percent silver is applied to a flatware metal form, usually nickel or brass, resulting in silverplated utensils—among the most popular.

Silverware   Another name for flatware, also categorizing all utensils.

Stainless steel   This ultra-durable metal is the material of choice for flatware and for knives. The top choice is 18 percent chrome and 8 percent nickel (marked as 18/8), which gives a better blend of durability and shine, or 18-10. This type of metal won't tarnish, fade, or corrode.

Stamped blades   For knives, this form is cut from a sheet of steel.

Steel   The metal of choice for light metal cookware like woks, with added strength and a light weight. Categories of steel on the market include "plain," "untreated," or "rolled."

Sterling silver   More expensive than silver-plated flatware, this heavier metal is not quite as durable as silver plating. This form is sometimes called "solid silver," but shouldn't be confused with 100 percent silver. Copper is a part of its blend for strength, and it is measured to a degree of at least 92.5 percent sterling silver.

Vermeil   A thin layer of gold applied to sterling flatware.

Place Settings

Four-piece place setting   The most common form for casual china, this set includes a dinner plate, bread and butter plate, salad/dessert plate, and a mug.

Five-piece place setting   The most common form for formal china, this set includes a dinner plate, bread and butter plate, salad/dessert plate, cup, and saucer.

Bone china   Considered the top form of china, it is fired at a hot temperature to create a white, glasslike appearance and a high level of durability. It's the addition of bone ash to the china mix that gives it that ultra-white appearance. Bone china is considered the best of the best.

Casual china   Another name for everyday dinnerware, available in four- and five-piece place servings.

Casual dinnerware   Not fine china, but rather everyday dishes and place settings. These types of dishes are often used the majority of the time and are dishwasher and microwave safe.

China   A roundup term encompassing a range of dinnerware, such as earthenware and fine china, but this term most directly refers to porcelain.

Completor set   The "extras" on a set table, including sugar bowl, creamer, salt and pepper shakers, and serving platters.

Dinnerware   The category for all place setting sets, including dinner plate, salad/dessert plate, bread plate, cup, and saucer. Some sets include a soup bowl and mug as part of the collection. This term may be used for both casual and formal sets.

Earthenware   A form of dinnerware made of fired clay, usually glazed, and often found as everyday china.

Formal china, or fine china   A collection of bone or porcelain china.

Ironstone   Also called Masonware, this form of earthenware is a porcelain or bone look-alike, but is heavier and more durable, not as fine as the authentics.

Porcelain   A top-quality china, lacking only the bone ash that is used in bone china, this durable form of china is among the most valuable and most popular available.

Stoneware   Made from a fortified clay with ground stone in the mix, then fired at a high temperature, this is a durable product. It can often be used in the oven, microwave, and dishwasher.

Vitrified ceramics   A glasslike form of ceramics, found to varying degrees of hardness and nonporous standards depending on the quality of the ceramic.

Index